# GHOSTS

## OF THE GREAT LAKES

## More Than Mere Legend

Megan Long

1st Edition: June 2003

Project Producers: Russell Floren, Barbara Chisholm and Andrea Gutsche
Editor: Barbra Chisholm
Cover and Design by: Andrea Gutsche

National Library of Canada Cataloguing in Publication

Printed in Canada

Long, Megan, 1975-
        Ghosts of the Great Lakes :
more than mere legend / by Megan Long.


Includes bibliographical references and index.
ISBN 1-882376-89-7
        I. Ghosts--Great Lakes Region. I. Title.


BF1472.G74L65 2003        133.1'0977
C2003-903111-X

We acknowledge the support of the Government of Ontario through the Ontario Media Development Corporation's Ontario Book Initiative.

# GHOSTS

## OF THE GREAT LAKES

## More Than Mere Legend

Megan Long

# Ghosts of the Great Lakes
## Location Map

∞

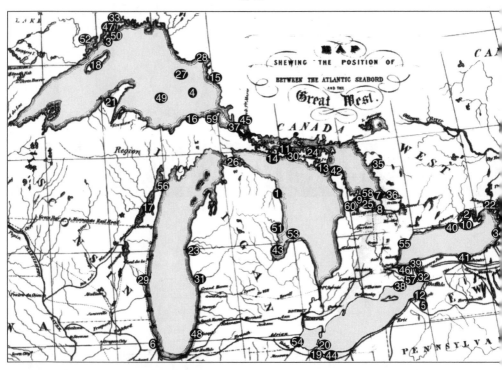

## Key ∞

| | | | |
|---|---|---|---|
| 1: Alpena | 17: Green Bay | 33: Nipigon | 49: Stannard Rock |
| 2: Belleville | 18: Isle Royale | 34: Oswego | 50: Talbot Island |
| 3: Bowman Island | 19: Johnson's Island | 35: Parry Sound | 51: Tawas Point |
| 4: Caribou Island | 20: Kelleys Island | 36: Penetang | 52: Thunder Bay |
| 5: Chautauqua County | 21: Keweenaw Peninsula | 37: Point aux Pins | (Port Arthur) (Fort William) |
| 6: Chicago | 22: Kingston | 38: Port Colborne | 53: Thunder Bay Island |
| 7: Christian Island | 23: Ludington | 39: Port Dalhousie | 54: Toledo |
| 8: Collingwood | 24: Manitoulin Island | 40: Presqu'ile | 55: Toronto |
| 9: Colpoy's Bay | 25: Meaford | 41: Rochester | 56: Washington Island |
| 10: Consecon | 26: Michilimackinac | 42: Russell Island | 57: Welland Canal |
| 11: Drummond Island | 27: Michipicoten Island | 43: Saginaw Bay | 58: White Cloud Island |
| 12: Dunkirk | 28: Michipicoten Harbour | 44: Sandusky | 59: Whitefish Point |
| 13: Fitzwilliam Island | 29: Milwaukee | 45: Sault Ste Marie | 60: Wiarton |
| 14: Fort Drummond | 30: Mississagi Strait | 46: St. Catharines | |
| 15: Gargantua | 31: Muskegon | 47: St. Ignace Island | |
| 16: Grand Marais | 32: Niagara River | 48: St. Joseph | |

# Contents

— ᎒ꙮ —

# Introduction

 ⭑⭑

Late at night, in the midst of a November storm, a sailor looks wearily over the water and glimpses something that shouldn't be there—a ghostly form gliding across the lake. Is it a figment of his imagination, or is it a ghost ship? The Great Lakes have a colorful past that spans hundreds of years and is filled with incredible stories, some more difficult to explain than others. From the far eastern shores of Lake Ontario all the way west to Lake Superior, this book reveals haunting and bizarre tales, whispers from the other side.

 In native cosmologies, much has always been attributed to forces beyond human control. Once Europeans arrived in the region, they experienced their own events that could not easily be explained. As early as 1679, French explorer René-Robert Cavelier Sieur de la Salle's barque, the *Griffon*, became the first reported ghost ship on the Great Lakes when it was lost on Lake Michigan. After the explorers and fur traders came European settlers extracting resources, working the land and establishing communities. This pressure increased the traffic on the Great Lakes waterways—the essential highway. The lakes were not easily tamed, however. Their waters have been known to swallow ships whole and never to reveal their remains. Can these losses always be attributed to human error or to the brutal storms that plague these inland seas, or are additional forces at work? One author, Hugh Cochrane, argues that the number of

The phantom ship is a reoc-current image in maritime lore.

mysterious events on a portion of Lake Ontario outdoes the famous Bermuda Triangle. "It is a strange place where ships, planes, and people vanish into thin air, where weird fogs and globes of light abound, where ominous waters shroud sinister events." [i]

Our journey through the ghostly goings-on of the Great Lakes includes haunted lighthouses, premonitions, the ghost of a forlorn lover, a powerful manitou, and prisoners of war who do not rest peace-fully—stories often relegated to "oddities" in historical accounts. This book sets out to bring together these stories that are passed down through generations so that they can be re-examined and remembered. Each story also reveals much about different aspects of Great Lakes his-tory. They are far from just tall tales; as with much folklore, they are often heavily based in truth. However, some argue that the stories cannot be considered fact, and should not be included in the history of the Lakes. In this volume, they are laid out with as much historical informa-tion as possible, to enable the reader to decide. Do these ghosts of the Great Lakes exist? And in what way might they have a place in history?

---------------- &⊙& ----------------

The Fox Sisters and Modern Spiritualism

Lily of the Prince George Hotel

The Disappearance of His Majesty's Vessel Speedy

Gibraltar Point Lighthouse

Watch Your Wake! The Hamilton and Scourge

# LAKE
# ONTARIO

*Maggie and Kate Fox, the two founders of modern Spiritualism. Author Susanna Moodie would later comment on Kate's haunting eyes, "the most beautiful eyes I ever saw in a human head. Not black, but a sort of dark purple. She is certainly a witch."*

# The Fox Sisters and Modern Spiritualism

In March of 1848 the Fox family began to hear strange sounds reverberating through their small house. There were eerie knocking noises emanating from the ceiling, doors and walls—some vibrated loudly enough to rattle bedsteads and tables. John Fox searched for the source of the knocks, but found nothing. The noises kept John and Margaret and their two youngest children, Margaretta (Maggie, 14) and Catherine (Kate, 11), awake at night to the point that Margaret complained, "we had been broken so much of our rest that I was almost sick." [1] On March 31st she ordered the family to bed before dark and commanded them to lie still and ignore the knocking sounds.

Whatever was making the sounds, however, was not to be ignored, and the raps piped up with steady noise. In her article in *American Heritage*, "They Spoke With the Dead," Barbara M. Weiber recounts what happened next. The two children were thrilled with the rappings. "Do as I do," challenged Kate as she snapped her fingers. There was a response of rapping in the same pattern. Maggie joined in, clapping her hands: "Count one, two, three, four." Four knocks responded. "Oh, Mother, I know what it is," Kate ventured, "Tomorrow is April Fool Day and someone is trying to fool us." In

*The youngest of the sisters, Kate Fox struggled with alcoholism throughout her life.*

later interviews Mrs. Fox would explain, "…I spoke and said to the noise, 'Count ten,' and it made ten strokes or noises… Then I asked the ages of my different children successively, and it gave a number of raps, corresponding to the ages of my children." She went further: "I then asked if it

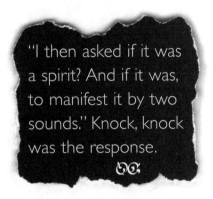

"I then asked if it was a spirit? And if it was, to manifest it by two sounds." Knock, knock was the response.

was a spirit? And if it was, to manifest it by two sounds." Knock, knock was the response. "I then asked if it was an injured spirit?… if it was injured in this house?… If the person was living that injured it?… I then ascertained, by the same method, that its remains were buried under the dwelling."

Apart from having this strange phenomenon visit their house, the Fox family was not a particularly unusual one. Until a few months before the rappings began, the Foxes lived in Consecon, Ontario, a small farming community southwest of Belleville. John Fox was a farmer and blacksmith and was not doing very well. Life looked more promising in New York, so the family moved to Hydesville, north of Newark. They rented a small house at the corner of Hydesville and Parker Road while their own home was being built. The Foxes had three other children besides Maggie and Kate—Elizabeth, Leah and Daniel—but they were grown up and had left home.

Margaret Fox's "conversation" with the mysterious rapping sounds that night convinced her that she was, in fact, communicating with some sort of spirit. She continued to ask questions of this spirit,

*LEFT Eldest sister Leah is accused of exploiting her sisters' gifts in order to elevate her own social status.*

which it would answer with knocking for yes and silence for no. In this manner she determined that it was the spirit of a 31-year-old man who had been dead for two years and was buried in the cellar. At around eight p.m. that evening John Fox summoned about a dozen neighbors to share in the bizarre show. According to David Chapin's article, "The Fox Sisters and the Mystery of Performance," Mary Redfield arrived on the scene to find that Margaret and the two girls "were much frightened." Another neighbor, Mr. Duesler, took over the questioning and learned more about the spirit: the man was a peddler who was murdered in the bedroom with a butcher knife that had slit his throat on a Tuesday five years earlier at midnight. His body was buried in the cellar ten feet below the surface. This gruesome end was all for the five hundred dollars he carried with him. The murderer was identified as a previous tenant of the house, John C. Bell, who was currently living in nearby Lyons, New York.

Over the next few days, hundreds of visitors came to the house to hear the mysterious knockings and find out more about the

LEFT *Maggie Fox originally produced the rapping sounds by tying apples to strings and bouncing them on the floor next to her bed.*

murder. Certainly if there had been foul play then the killer should be incarcerated! The knockings could not be heard during the day, but as soon as darkness returned, the spirit resumed its communication and the eager community members asked their questions. They narrowed down the area in the cellar where the body had been buried and went to work looking for the human remains that would prove or disprove the existence of this spirit. Before they reached four feet, however, they struck water and had to give up the dig.

Despite this setback, there were plenty of other stories around to lend weight to the claims. Other tenants of the house came forward with their own accounts of strange noises, and one of John Bell's employees claimed to have seen signs of digging in the cellar at the time of the alleged murder. She also claimed that the digging appeared only a few days after a peddler had visited the home and then mysteriously disappeared. None of the allegations against Mr. Bell could be proven, and charges were never brought against him. However, some accounts note that human bones were later found in the cellar.

LEFT Kate Fox. Kate's older sister Leah brought her to Rochester, where news of the sisters' gifts spread rapidly.

March 31, 1848, became regarded as the birthdate of a movement called Spiritualism, which Maggie and Kate are credited with beginning. In the days and weeks following March 31st it became obvious that the spirit was only communicating while Maggie or Kate were present, and the sisters became known as mediums. News of their strange powers spread, and the girls began to perform for small groups in private homes. In May, the news reached their older sister Leah in Rochester. Curious, Leah booked passage on a packet boat to Newark. When she arrived and saw what was happening in the presence of her sisters, she sprang into action. Sensing opportunity, Leah became instrumental in promoting the popularity of her sisters' gifts, and she even became a medium herself. She convinced her mother to let her take Kate back to Rochester with her, reasoning that separating the girls might stop the knocking. It didn't, and she explained in a book she later wrote that the spirits followed them to Rochester. Not only did they follow them, but the sounds also became louder; and, while the women were asleep, the spirits moved beds in the house and threw objects in the air.

During the 1830s and '40s, a religious revival, called by some the Second Great Awakening, was in full swing in the Rochester area.

These revivalists advocated the free moral agency of Christians and the ability of individuals to influence their own salvation. A group of revivalists looked favorably upon the Fox sisters' ability to communicate with the dead, and Leah skillfully promoted the rappings as part of this age of progressive reform.[ii] Some of the first seances that the sisters performed were for prominent Hicksite Quakers and evangelical Methodists. These new relationships lifted Leah into the middle-class clique that she had longed to join. The Fox sisters were coddled and encouraged by these communities and soon were traveling to western New York to hold seances.

In the fall of 1849, Maggie and Leah held a demonstration of the rappings in Corinthian Hall, the largest hall in Rochester. This was the first time, but certainly not the last, that the Foxes

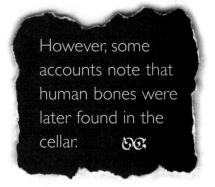

However, some accounts note that human bones were later found in the cellar.

would charge admission for their services. Newspaper advertisements read: "Let the citizens of Rochester embrace this opportunity of investigating the whole matter, and see if those engaged in laying it before the public are deceived, or are deceiving others, and if neither, account for these truly wonderful manifestations...." And investigate they did. Audience members put the girls to the test, and at the end of each performance, they even elected a committee to examine the girls more closely. Chosen audience members placed the girls' feet in different positions, stood the sisters on glass plates and even listened

In 1850, the Fox sisters moved to New York City, where they held seances and even appeared at P.T. Barnum's American Museum.

to their lungs with stethoscopes, but they could not determine how Maggie and Leah might be making the noises. Eliab Capron, who delivered a lecture on the history of spirit rapping at the performances, wrote that "a committee of ladies... took the young women into a room, disrobed them, and examined their persons and clothing." Still, they could not find fault with the Foxes.

These performances in Rochester launched the Foxes into the national spotlight. The sisters moved to New York City, where they conducted seances for prominent New Yorkers. With the discovery of many other mediums, Spiritualism and spirit rapping grew in the United States and Britain. There was, of course, also skepticism. Some doctors and scientists hypothesized that the sisters made the knocking noises by cracking their toes—a theory called "toe-ology." Even more damaging to the movement was the announcement by a trio of Buffalo doctors that "an instance has fallen under our observation, which demonstrates the fact, that noises precisely identified with the *spiritual rappings* may be produced in the *knee joint.*"[iii] These same doctors examined the sisters in 1851 and pronounced themselves victorious, as no raps occurred when the sisters' knees were restricted. The spiritualists fought back, saying that the environment was too hostile for the spirits to come forth. Despite the doctors' conclusions, the girls' celebrity continued to grow.

Even the most skeptical were intrigued. In the fall of 1855, Canadian pioneer and author Susanna Moodie wrote to her British publisher, Richard Bentley:

> I have had several visits from Miss Kate Fox the celebrated Spirit Rapper, who is a very lovely intellectual looking girl, with the most beautiful eyes I ever saw in a human head. Not black, but a sort of dark purple. She is certainly a witch, for you cannot help looking into the dreamy depths of those sweet violet eyes till you feel magnetized by them… I do not believe that the raps are produced by spirits that have been of this world, but I cannot believe that she, with her pure spiritual face is capable of deceiving. She certainly does not procure these mysterious sounds by foot or hand, and though I cannot help thinking they emanate from her mind and that she is herself the spirit, I believe she is perfectly unconscious of it herself.[iv]

Pioneer author Susanna Moodie visited with Kate Fox in the fall of 1855 and was convinced that she was truly a medium.

On one occasion, Moodie even tested Kate:

I thought I would puzzle them [the spirits], and ask for them to rap out my father's name, the date of his birth and death, which was rather a singular one from the constant recurrence of one figure. He was born Dec. 8th. I did not know myself in what year, was 58 when he died, which happened the 18th of May 1818. To my astonishment all this was rapped out. His name. The disease of which he died (gout in the stomach) and the city (Norwich), where he died. The question being mental could not have been guessed by any person of common powers. But she may be Clairvoyant, and able to read unwritten thoughts. I have not time just now to give you more on this subject, and though still a great skeptic as to the spiritual nature of the thing, the intelligence conveyed is unaccountable. Can such a thing as witchcraft really exist? Or possession by evil spirits? I am bewildered and know not what to answer. [vi]

Moodie eventually admitted to Bentley that she accepted that spirit rapping was a real phenomenon.

*ABOVE In the 1850s, the Foxes began to charge for their seances. Their rates were one dollar per person per hour or five dollars for a private seance for two or more people.*

While the life of a medium had its glamor, it by no means ensured happiness. Maggie met and fell in love with Dr. Elisa Kent Kane, a prominent physician and Arctic explorer. Kane disapproved of Maggie's spirit rapping and begged her to "come clean." [vii] Before he left on a two-year voyage to the Arctic in search of missing British explorer John Franklin, Kane convinced Maggie to give up her public spirit rapping and to move to Pennsylvania to live under the supervision of his relatives. She was desperately lonely during his absence;

then, a few years after Kane returned home, he left again, this time for England. Sadly, on his return voyage, Kane grew ill and had to disembark at Havana, Cuba, where he died, leaving Maggie to deal with his disapproving family. Maggie contended that she and Kane had been married in a small, private ceremony before he left, but Kane's family publicly denied this and even stopped paying Maggie the small annuity that was keeping her afloat. She did keep her promise to Kane, however, and retired from spirit rapping, converting to Roman Catholicism in 1858.

Older sister Leah also retired and married her third husband, wealthy businessman and spiritualist Daniel Underhill. Kate continued to hold seances. The year 1865 brought another blow to the sisters—their parents both died. Maggie and Kate were known to have problems with alcoholism, but this news sent them spiraling. In hopes of leaving her addiction behind, Kate moved to England, where she married a wealthy barrister and spiritualist, Henry D. Jencken, and bore two children. When Jencken died in the early 1880s, Kate returned to the United States with her children, her alcoholism clearly more serious than when she left. Meanwhile, Maggie was desperate for money and had returned to spirit rapping.

In March 1888, spiritualists celebrated their 40th anniversary. In October of that same year, Maggie and Kate delivered a bombshell to their followers. On stage at the New York Academy of Music, Maggie pronounced, "I am here tonight as one of the founders of Spiritualism, to denounce it as an absolute falsehood from beginning to end, as the flimsiest of superstitions, the most wicked blasphemy known to the world." [viii] She then removed her right shoe and placed her bare foot on a stool and demonstrated the sharp rapping sounds she could make with the first joint of her big toe that had led so many followers to believe they were the words of long-dead spirits. Finally, the truth was out!

However, that was not the end of Spiritualism; in fact, the sisters later denounced their own confessions. In 1916, a spiritualist bought the Hydesville cottage where the rappings first began and transported it to a spiritualist camp in Chautauqua County, western New York State, where it was used for seances. Nearly forty years after Maggie's revelation, a wealthy Rochester spiritualist, M.E. Cadwallader, erected a granite marker at the sight of the house where the raps were first heard. It reads:

> The Birthplace of
> MODERN SPIRITUALISM
> Upon This Site Stood
> The Hydesville Cottage
> The Home of the
> FOX SISTERS
> Through Whose Mediumship Communications
> With the Spirit World was Established
> March 31, 1848
> There Is No Death
> There Is No Dead
> Placed Here by M. E. Cadwallader
> Dec. 5, 1927

*The British government negotiated with the Mississauga Indians to obtain the land at what is now Kingston. United Empire Loyalists who came from the American colonies after the American Revolution settled here. Lawrence Herchmer was among the first Loyalists to bring his family to Kingston. He purchased land near the waterfront and built a home where the Prince George Hotel now stands.*

# Lily of the Prince George Hotel

ᘒᘓ

The story of the Prince George Hotel in Kingston, Ontario, has all the elements of a classic ghost tale: a historic building, a secret love and a tragic death. Standing on the current hotel site was a two-storey house built by the Herchmer family, wealthy United Empire Loyalists who were among the first settlers to own and operate a business on the waterfront. In the early 1800s, the Kingston waterfront was rough and tumble, dotted with warehouses for furs, agricultural products and imported goods. Arriving sailors would spend a few nights on the town, patronizing the selection of saloons and houses of ill repute.

Legend has it that the Herchmers' youngest daughter, Lily, known to be lovely if a bit naive, had an illicit affair with one of the sailors who frequented the port. To signal her secret lover, Lily took to hanging a lantern in her bedroom window. One windy night, however, Lily fell asleep while the lantern was burning, and sparks ignited the room. Within moments, a fire was raging, and Lily was killed. (A completely different version of the story reports that Lily watched from her bedroom window as her lover's ship sank in the harbor, but this version is not as often repeated.)

Lily's father, Lawrence Herchmer, died in 1819, leaving the house to his wife Elizabeth, who lived there until 1840. Her son-in-

*Kingston, c.1850. Kingston's waterfront was bustling in the early 1800s. From her room, Lily Herchmer had a view of the incoming ships.*

law, John McPherson, then took over the property. He transformed the building, then known as the John McPherson House, into shops, warehouse space and saloons. During his tenure, there was another major fire, and the building underwent further renovations. In 1918 the building became the Prince George Hotel. Remarkably, it stayed in the Herchmer family until 1951. The building was refurbished several more times over the years. In 1978, owner Patrick Rousseau hired an architect (coincidentally named Lily Inglis) to add new lounges and to remodel the Victorian porch, central tower and hotel rooms. In the current incarnation, Monte's Cigar and Martini Lounge, the British pub the Old Speckled Hen, and the Irish pub Tir na N'Og occupy the main floor, and there are 26 hotel rooms on the two floors above.

With so many changes, it may seem surprising that Lily could find her way around the hotel, but many report that she has managed to maintain a presence. She is said to dwell on the third floor in Room 304, approximately where her bedroom was located in the original Herchmer home. The room still offers an excellent view of the harbor. Several guests claim to have encountered Lily while staying in the room. One desk clerk has recounted the experience of an elderly couple: "They were sleeping in one of the two double beds in the room.

The couple awoke to see the second double bed levitating three feet off the floor. The gentleman wanted to know if that was normal!"[i] Many have also reported a shadowy form that appears in the hallways. Lily has also been said to unlock room doors, and her footsteps have been heard in the basement. From the Irish pub have come reports of the apparition of a sailor and a young woman—perhaps Lily and her lover, or perhaps an effect of the Guinness.

Still another mystery shrouding the Prince George Hotel may be linked to Lily Herchmer. According to members of the staff, the tower light has been known to spontaneously turn itself on at night, even though the breaker shows the power to that light to be switched off.[ii] Perhaps this is Lily's modern-day method of signaling to her forlorn sailor, who she imagines still awaits.

The Prince George Hotel has operated at the site since Confederation.

The *Speedy* took with it most members of the young government of Upper Canada.

# The Disappearance of His Majesty's Vessel Speedy

Each of the Great Lakes has remarkable unexplained phenomena, but Lake Ontario is home to some of the most puzzling disappearances anywhere in the world. An area at the eastern end of the lake, called the Marysburgh Vortex, is said to rival the Bermuda Triangle in its strange disappearances.[i] Ships, people and planes have all gone missing without a trace. Perhaps the most intriguing of these stories is that of the government of Upper Canada's schooner *Speedy*. It begins with a murder, moves on to unexplained forces and dark premonitions and ends with a mystery that remains unsolved almost two hundred years later!

The last voyage of the *Speedy* took place in the fall of 1804, and it is linked to a case of questionable justice. In the frontier area north of Presqu'ile, at the eastern end of Lake Ontario, an Ojibwa man named Ogetonicut allegedly murdered white settler John Sharp. The murder was apparently in retaliation for the killing of Ogetonicut's brother, Whistling Duck, by another white settler, Samuel Cozens. Although Cozens escaped justice, the colonial body made every effort to ensure that Ogetonicut was captured and prosecuted. [ii]

Massive waves battered the lakeshores on the night the *Speedy* went missing. Worried citizens set bonfires in an attempt to lead the ship to safety.

Ogetonicut was apprehended in the summer of 1804 at what is now known as Toronto Island, and a trial was scheduled for the fall. The law of the time required that trials be carried out in the same district in which the crime allegedly took place. The *Speedy* was called into service to transport the prisoner, Judge Thomas Cochrane and other court officials east to Presqu'ile, where Ogetonicut was to be tried and hanged at a temporary courthouse (apparently the outcome of the trial was a foregone conclusion). The occasion of the trip was also to be used to transport government dignitaries attending a ceremony to establish the new town of Newcastle, which happened to be at the site of the trial.

One Sunday in November, the various court officials, government dignitaries, the prisoner and a few passengers boarded the *Speedy* at York (now Toronto) for the 100-mile (160-km) trip to Presqu'ile.

Captain Richardson was originally scheduled to make the voyage, but he felt a strange feeling of dread about the trip and refused to sail.

The *Speedy* had the unusual distinction of having two captains, Thomas Paxton and James Richardson. Captain Richardson was originally scheduled to make the voyage, but he felt a strange feeling of dread about the trip and refused to sail. He cautioned the others in the party that something was amiss. Even though the command of the *Speedy* was turned over to Captain Paxton, Captain Richardson kept up his warnings until the ship cast off. The vessel was scheduled to pick up witnesses for the trial along the way, but a strong sense of foreboding convinced those people to take the more difficult overland route to Presqu'ile rather than sail. What was it that was warning them away from the *Speedy*?

Later that evening the government vessel came up against an unexpected and brutal November storm. Along the shore, many who knew the *Speedy* was on the water peered through the darkness, hoping to catch sight of the vessel. Some had never seen such a violent storm on Lake Ontario. They lit bonfires to lead the *Speedy* to safety, but Captain Paxton did not seek shelter that night. Was he so confident in his ship that he was certain they would reach their destination without incident? This is hard to imagine, as despite the *Speedy* being only eight years old, dry rot had set in, and the hull needed constant attention.[iii] Those who glimpsed the ship that night said it appeared to be out of control. In fact, when last seen, the *Speedy* was heading directly for a dangerous rock formation near Presqu'ile.

This rock formation has an even more curious story. Earlier that spring, when a crewmember of the *Lady Mary* spotted what appeared to be a small, unknown shoal at the entrance to the bay at Presqu'ile, Captain Charles Selleck and a few others lowered a dinghy and rowed over for a closer look. It was true: just under the surface there was a rock about forty feet square. Soundings revealed that the lake bottom dropped straight down for 300 feet (118m) all around the rock. This was a surprise, as it was previously believed that these waters were quite shallow. To be sure, they took more soundings, all of which confirmed the earlier results. Over the next few months, curiosity brought many others to the strange rock to take their own soundings. One of those who visited the site that summer, Captain Paxton was well aware of the shoal's danger to navigation.

The morning after the horrendous storm, the *Speedy* was nowhere to be found. Days went by without even a sign of the vessel ever having been there. Eventually, authorities decided to drag the area around the rock formation. No trace was found, but even stranger, there was no sign of the rock formation—it had disappeared! Even more confusing, the surrounding deep waters were now shallow and sandy. His Majesty's Vessel, along with the accused and the prosecutors aboard, was never found, and no one has yet solved the mystery.

TOP The Gibraltar Point Lighthouse had an oil lantern that could be seen for about seven miles (11.2km) and burned about 200 gallons of sperm whale oil each year. LOWER The lighthouse, seen right, and a military post were built on the peninsula that would later become Toronto Island.

# Murder at Gibraltar Point Lighthouse

───────────── ☙ℰ❧ ─────────────

The story of this fabled lighthouse begins in 1793, when Colonel John Graves Simcoe ordered the fortification of the harbor at York (now Toronto). This included building two stone houses and a guard-house on Gibraltar Point to defend against American naval invasion. It also included building a lighthouse nearby. At the time, these sites were on a peninsula that jutted out from the mainland and curved around to the west to form the south flank of the harbor. In 1858, however, a tremendous storm washed away tons of sand and created a channel, turning the peninsula into Toronto Island. The lighthouse still remains; in fact, it is the oldest historical landmark in Toronto still at its original site. But it is now landlocked: silt has collected along the shore and moved the shoreline well out. Also stranded at the light is one of Toronto's most famous ghosts, lightkeeper John Paul Radelmüller.

Simcoe chose a site for the lighthouse in April 1808, and before long, a fixed light was beaming out from atop a tapered stone tower. Radelmüller (also called Muller) was its first keeper. He was reportedly dedicated and fastidious, cleaning the lantern lens each

ABOVE  Map of Toronto Island showing its original formation as a series of sand-bars and marshes at the end of a long peninsula. The locations of a military outpost and lighthouse are shown. INSET  John Graves Simcoe and wife Elizabeth. Simcoe arrived in 1793 and ordered the building of a lighthouse to aid the water traffic in and out of the harbor. By the early 1800s, the town of York had reached 700 inhabitants.

morning and keeping the lighthouse in perfect order. He was also known around Fort York and further afield for his skill in brewing beer, a skill he had brought from his native Germany. He made the best pilsner on the lake, and he was always willing to share it with friends and strangers who came to visit. It was this generosity that may have attracted trouble and caused his disappearance.

Legend has it that one January night in 1815, two or three inebriated soldiers from the fort showed up at his home and demanded beer. Concerned that they were already quite drunk, Radelmüller tried to convince them to return to the fort or stay at the light with him until the alcohol wore off. "Hand over the beer!" one of the soldiers yelled in reply. He was rumored to be an imposing brute who sported a scar down one cheek. Radelmüller stood his ground, but the soldier

Fort York. Drinking was such a common problem among soldiers that on payday, the military authorities posted an extra night guard to ensure that soldiers made it back to their barracks.

grabbed a chunk of firewood and brandished it above his head while continuing his verbal threats.

Several differing accounts have been recorded of the subsequent events. Most agree that Radelmüller refused the soldiers again and paid for it with his life. Some accounts say that the soldiers killed him by striking him on the head with the firewood; then, still enraged, they dragged him to the top of the tower and threw his limp body off. Others say that he was beaten to death with the wood and the soldiers' belts. Either way, the keeper was never seen again. Rumors of foul play circulated at Fort York, but no one had convincing evidence to support any of the theories. A new lightkeeper was appointed, and life at the lighthouse continued.

Almost eighty years later, keeper George Durnam made a startling discovery. While digging near the light in 1893, he came across human bones. The authorities concluded that they were Radelmüller's remains and that he had indeed been murdered! Later on, Durnam came forward with stories about a ghostly presence at the light. On dark, foggy nights he had heard Radelmüller's moans and seen his ghost searching the site for his murderers. A newspaper reporter decided to disprove Durnam's claims and spent the night at the light. What he experienced did nothing to debunk the ghost myth, however. That evening he inspected the entire lighthouse. A few hours later, he made the same rounds. This time he found that someone had brushed up against the inside wall of the light and left a mark in the plaster and a fine white powder underneath it on the stairs—but no one had been in the lighthouse since his inspection. The reporter swept up the plaster, shuddering to himself. When he returned later there was more plaster residue on the stairs. Was it Radelmüller who was walking up the stairs to check on his light? Numerous other reports include sightings of him, hearing him being dragged up the stairs, and other unaccountable noises.

The Gibraltar Point lighthouse remained in service for 150 years until being replaced by a small tower in 1958. The original 52-foot (15.6-m) tapered tower, with its impressive 6-foot (1.8-m)-thick stone walls, is the oldest standing lighthouse on the Great Lakes. Many still believe that the tower remains the home of murdered lightkeeper Radelmüller. Why does he remain at the lighthouse? Is it his unsolved murder that refuses to let his spirit rest?

ABOVE George Durnam (right) discovered human bones buried near the lighthouse in 1893. Here a reporter is interviewing him about the discovery. Note the painting of the lighthouse at the far right. FAR LEFT Gibraltar Point Lighthouse, the oldest standing lighthouse on the Great Lakes, was discontinued in the 1950s.

ABOVE Peter Rindlisbacher's painting of the *Scourge*. The *Scourge* was launched as the Royal Navy schooner *Lord Nelson*. The United Nations has declared the *Hamilton* and *Scourge* wrecks World Heritage Sites, as they are two of the best surviving examples of warships from their era in the world.

# Watch Your Wake!
# The Hamilton & Scourge

&#1256;&#1256;

On the night of August 7, 1813, a fleet of American naval schooners lay on the calm lake, their wooden decks creaking as the boats swayed. The schooners were a little west of the mouth of the Niagara River, close to St. Catharines, Ontario. It was the thick of the War of 1812, and lying not far to the north was the British fleet. During the day the two sides had been maneuvering for position, but they had not exchanged fire. As darkness fell, American Commodore Isaac Chauncey pulled his flotilla in close to ensure that none were cut off from the rest during the night. On the American schooner *Scourge*, Captain Osgood ordered the sweeps (large oars) pulled in for the night, but not secured in case the British attacked under the cover of night. The sailors were to stay on deck to be at the ready. Most of the crew drifted off to sleep, lulled by the rhythmic slapping of the limp canvas. The stars twinkled in the clear sky.

Ned Myers of the *Scourge* was napping by his gun when large drops of rain began hitting his face. Tom Goldsmith awoke at the

Artist Duncan Macpherson's painting of the *Hamilton* and *Scourge* (in background). Originally named the *Diana*, the *Hamilton* was built at Oswego, New York, in 1809 for merchant Matthew McNair. On October 12, 1812, Captain Chauncey bought the ship and added it to his squadron. The name was changed to *Hamilton* in honor of the Secretary of the American Navy, Paul Hamilton.

same time, and Myers asked if he would like a nip from a bottle that was below in a mess chest. Another crewmate piped up that he wouldn't mind a nip himself, and Myers made his way to the forward hatch. In a later interview, Myers recalled the following moments:

> All this took half a minute, perhaps. I now remember to have heard a strange rushing noise to windward as I went towards the forward hatch, though it made no impression on me at the time.... One hand was on the bitts, and a foot was on the ladder, when a flash of lightning almost blinded me. The thunder came at the next instant, and with it a rushing of winds that fairly smothered the clap.

More men awoke from their slumber and raced to pull down the sails. Lightning strikes lit up the night, and gusts hammered the *Scourge*. Then the unthinkable happened. A gust hit with such intensity that it knocked the schooner over. The *Scourge* sank within minutes.

Much of the crew, trapped by the heavy guns as they slid across the deck, went down with the ship. Myers and some others were fortunate to have been flung in the water. Myers found the *Scourge's* tender, and by calling out to his crewmates, he managed to locate and drag seven other men in. The survivors began to row, but they were unsure of their direction, only catching glimpses of their surroundings in flashes of lightning. The men feared that the enemy fleet had moved in during the squall and hoped they were not rowing into danger. Thankfully, they came upon the American schooner *Julia* and were welcomed aboard.

ABOVE American Commodore Isaac Chauncey pulled his flotilla in close to ensure that none of his ships were cut off from the rest during the night.

The captain immediately sent out a boat to search for other survivors. Four men were found, but they were not from the *Scourge*; the American schooner *Hamilton* had also fallen victim to the squall! The survivors were given warm, dry clothes and ordered below deck to recover. The next morning the American fleet regrouped and learned that another

The American schooner *Julia* (far left) rescued some survivors from the *Scourge* disaster. On August 10, 1813, the British captured the *Julia* and the *Growler* (far right). In the heat of that battle, the *Julia* ran so close to shore that soundings revealed it to be sailing in only 12 feet of water.

vessel, the *Governor Tompkins*, had rescued four more of the *Hamilton's* crew, bringing the total number of survivors to 16. Myers estimated that there were "near a hundred souls" on board the two schooners. The next morning the remaining fleet searched the area and found relics of the disaster—sponges, hats, etc.—but no more survivors.

Now the *Hamilton* and *Scourge* (112 feet [34m] and 110 feet [33m] long respectively) lie in a bed of silt clay at the mouth of the Niagara River in about 300 feet (90m) of water. Preserved in pristine condition by the dark, ice-cold waters of Lake Ontario, they are considered to be two of the best examples of nineteenth-century warships extant in the world and have been designated World Heritage Sites by the United Nations. Sabers still lie where the crews dropped them, and skeletons litter the hulls. The schooners and their crews lay undisturbed for about 160 years, their whereabouts long forgotten, until Dr. Daniel A. Nelson (a dentist from St. Catharines, Ontario, and an amateur archaeologist) took up the cause to locate the wrecks. He used the logbook from British Commodore Sir James Lucas Yeo's ship, *Wolfe*, to predict the likely position of the vessels, and in 1971 joined forces with the Royal Ontario Museum in initiating the *Hamilton-Scourge* Project. Using a magnetometer and side-scan sonar, a likely mass was located, and finally, in 1975, researchers had their first view of the *Hamilton* and *Scourge*, upright on the lake floor, each with its masts intact. Subsequently, several groups have photographed the two wrecks, including divers from Jacques Cousteau's team, the *Hamilton-Scourge* Foundation and the National Geographic Society.

Sabers still lie where the crews dropped them, and skeletons litter the hulls.

Old-timers on Lake Ontario needed no photographs or video footage of the ships to remember their fate. Legend has it that now and again, when the lake is covered in mist, the two schooners can be seen sailing again. In some descriptions, the vessels are under full sail, and the crew on deck are illuminated by lanterns hung from the rigging. As suddenly as the storm that originally felled them, the schooners are seen to shake from the force of an invisible squall. As they succumb and disappear into the black water, the screams of drowning men echo across the lake. Some crews were terrified of these phantom ships, believing that if one crossed their wake it could mean death for someone on board.[i] In 1942, several men on the steamer *Cayuga* reported seeing the strange re-enactment. The schooners crossed the wake of the steamer at dusk, horrifying the ship's steward. He repeated the story to his crewmates, and by morning he was dead. Sailors take heed—the ghosts of the *Hamilton* and *Scourge* are not to be ignored.

---  &#x2767;  ---

The Black Dog of Lake Erie

Farewell to Johnson's Island

Kelleys Island Quarrymen

The Convict Ship Success

# LAKE
# ERIE

Some sailors believed that the Black Dog of Lake Erie was the ghost of a Newfoundland who was trapped and died in the Welland Canal.

# The Black Dog
# Of Lake Erie

⚮

"May the Black Dog of Lake Erie cross your deck," spat the drunken mate of the schooner *Azimuth*. The curse was a serious offence, and the captain lunged at him, beating him to the ground. Pulling the man back to his knees and aiming a fist at his face, the captain yelled, "Take it off, take it off, or your own mother will never know the look of your face." Trembling, the mate agreed to remove the curse. The captain demoted the mate to work in the foc'sle. The mate pleaded that he was "only foolin'", but the enraged captain continued. "By cracky, if I told the boys you'd threatened the Black Dog, they'd tear you limb from tree. To think of the blather of the likes of you scattering the *Azimuth* and her crowd along the front of some man's farm some dirty night! Take shame to yourself for thinking of it."

This story of the *Azimuth's* captain and mate was retold in a 1931 article in the *Toronto Telegram*.[i] The *Azimuth* continued to sail the lakes for years after this curse, but the captain's anger was certainly justified. The sailor had flirted with disaster when he spoke about the Black Dog of Lake Erie. The legendary mongrel was said to be the

While the crew was readying the *Mary Jane* for cast-off, a shaggy black Newfoundland was seen on the port side. Was it the Black Dog of Lake Erie?

ghost of a Newfoundland who died in the Welland Canal locks. The dog fell overboard from a schooner, and the cruel sailors jeered as it struggled and eventually drowned. Revenge was swift, however. Soon afterwards, the vessel became jammed in the lock. When it was finally freed, the body of the dead Newfoundland was found stuck behind the lock gates, where it had impeded the ship's progress. The curse followed the schooner for the rest of its days, and in the years that followed, the Black Dog took vengeance on other vessels on Lake Erie. The story goes that the ghost of the dog would appear momentarily on the deck of a ship, then disappear over the rail. Such a sighting was followed by certain disaster for the vessel.

The dark beast was blamed for, among others, the early disappearances of the *Mary Jane* and the *C. T. Jenkins*. The legend of the *Mary Jane* begins one calm, sunny day in Port Colborne, Ontario. The 135-foot (40.5-m) schooner was tied at dock with a full load of cedar posts, awaiting a favorable wind for sailing on Lake Erie. Finally, a slight breeze tickled the sails, and the schooner was ready to be towed out of port. As the *Mary Jane* pushed off, a massive black Newfoundland "with lolling tongue and eyes like coals of fire" was seen on the port deck amongst the cedar posts.[ii] It trotted across the cargo and leapt ashore from the starboard side, much to the astonishment of the crew and those watching from the dock. "Now, where did that brute come from?" asked Tinny Garner, who worked the elevator at Port Colborne. How could the dog have climbed up the side of the boat from the water? And where had it disappeared to? "He just seemed to touch the dock and go outa sight," said Tinny, suspicious that this strange dog was the famous Black Dog of Lake Erie. [iii]

The dog would appear momentarily on the deck of a ship, then disappear over the rail. Such a sighting was followed by certain disaster for the vessel.

The breeze soon died, and the schooner bobbed in the afternoon sun between Port Colborne and the Mohawk Lighthouse. Workers from the Port Colborne elevator saw the *Mary Jane* as they came out for lunch at noon, but, oddly, when they returned to work an hour later, the vessel was nowhere to be seen. There had been no wind during the hour, and no one had seen it in distress—the *Mary Jane* had simply disappeared. The schooner and crew were never seen again.

That's how the legend goes. Some historians contend, however, that the story has taken on mythic proportions over the generations and that some of the basic facts about the disappearance of the schooner have become skewed. The legend reads that the vessel was lost on a sunny summer day, when, in fact, the *Mary Jane* left Port Colborne on a dark and rainy November day in 1881. The *Detroit Free Press* reported the loss a week later, along with the loss of the schooner *E.P. Dorr*. "The Canadian barquentine *Mary Jane* left the Welland canal... on the same day when the *Dorr* was last seen, and likely wrecked the same night, which was very stormy, with snow squalls."

Also lost over time was the fact that the *Mary Jane's* deckload was discovered at about the same time as the cargo of the Dorr was found, contrary to the story, which claims that no trace was ever found of the vessel. The *Globe of Buffalo* reported on November 23, 1881: "The schooner *Mary Jane*, of St. Catharines, was wrecked five miles east of Dunkirk. There are no signs of the crew. The vessel is a total wreck. Boxes marked *Mary Jane* were coming ashore near Dunkirk." Clearly, facts have been embellished, but does this mean the Black Dog was not involved in the disaster?

The *C. T. Jenkins* was yet another schooner that purportedly fell to the Black Dog. During the middle watch on a quiet night sail, the helmsman of the *Jenkins* let out a blood-curdling yell, waking every soul on board. Stumbling from their beds, they peered onto the deck to see the terrified man blurt out, "The Black Dog! It came up over the weather rail in the moonlight, all black and bristling, and not a hair of it wet, and it walked across the deck and over the lee rail and into the lake without a splash." The bewildered crew looked at each other, but Captain John Brown suspected that hooch was to blame for the helmsman's vision. Digging out a flask from the sailor's pocket, he threw it overboard. "See if this makes a splash! Cook, make him some coffee, strong enough to float the kedge anchor! And you, blank you, get to your bunk and keep your conversation hatch on as soon as you've stowed what the cook gives you, see?" yelled the captain, punctuating his anger with a swift kick at the man.[iv]

When the helmsman emerged from his stupor, the memory of the Black Dog was still with him. The *Jenkins* was being towed into Port Colborne to prepare for the trip through the canal to Lake Ontario. On shore, he found a captive audience as the Canadian rye flowed. By the third round, the dog had grown to mammoth proportions. When the helmsman returned to the schooner he was near tears and begged his fellow crewmates to leave the ship and save themselves from the dreaded curse. Captain Brown hurled the man off the boat, chucking his bag after him, but the dismissed helmsman was not so easily dissuaded. As the schooner worked its way through the Welland Canal, he followed the *Jenkins* from shore. Each time the boat arrived at a lock, he pleaded with the crew to leave the doomed vessel. Although he was repeatedly driven away, by the time the *Jenkins* arrived in Port Dalhousie, the crew was on edge.

Sensing a mutiny, Captain Brown was anxious to set off. The *Jenkins* sailed into Lake Ontario with a steady breeze that blew hard through the night, but, reportedly, not hard enough to cause problems for the vessel. Still, the schooner did not reach port at Oswego. Tugs were sent to search for the missing vessel, but they found no trace. As though to corroborate the helmsman's fears, a farmer at Sheldon's Point to the west of Oswego saw a strange black dog come ashore. The dog had dark black hair that clung to its body, and it dragged its hind legs as though they were paralyzed. It disappeared as quickly as it had appeared. Had the Black Dog of Lake Erie struck again?

TOP The Johnson's Island prisoner-of-war camp included barracks, headquarters for officers of the guard, a prison hospital, a sutler's store, the Bull Pen (an enclosed area for outdoor recreation) and a burial ground. LOWER The 13 barracks (one seen right) were so poorly insulated that the icy winds of Lake Erie winters cut right through the walls and the men's light clothing. Many prisoners contracted pneumonia.

# Farewell to Johnson's Island

꒰ꗃ꒱

Hoarse-sounding billows of white-capped lake
That 'gainst the barriers of our hated prison break,
Farewell! Farewell; thou giant inland sea;
Thou too, subservest the modest of tyranny—
Girding this isle, washing its lonely shore.
With moaning echoes of thy melancholy roar.
Farewell, thou lake! Farewell, thou inhospitable land!
Thou hast the curses of this patriot band—
All, save the spot, the holy sacred bed,
Where rest in peace our Southern warriors dead.

A parting soldier etched this bitter farewell on the walls that had imprisoned him for untold months. During the American Civil War, Confederate prisoners of war were held captive on small Johnson's Island, a few miles offshore from Sandusky, Ohio. From 1861 to 1865, the prison held between 10,000 and 15,000 Southerners—men unaccustomed to the driving snow and ice of a Lake Erie winter. Most managed to endure these harsh days and the boredom of prison life. In fact, some might say the spirits of these

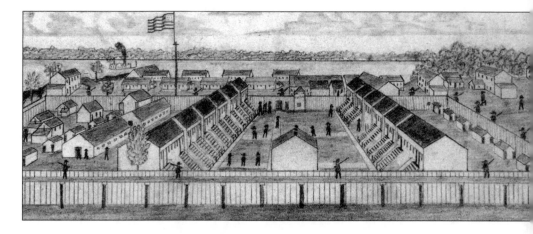

Covering 40 acres, the camp held as many as 3,000 prisoners during the Civil War. Few dared escaped over the 14-foot-high walls.

men were so resilient that those who died and were buried in the prison cemetery (206 in all) never really rested in peace. These souls are said to haunt Johnson's Island during the strongest of Erie's winter gales.

Back in 1852, a man named Leonard Johnson bought the 300-acre island and renamed it after himself. He founded a lime kiln and a quarry here, and during the Civil War leased 40 acres of land to the Union government for the building of Johnson's Prison. Prisoners of war destined for this island would first arrive by train in Sandusky, where townspeople called them murderers and thieves and taunted them mercilessly. The prisoners were then put on a ferry for the island. En route they would pass the imposing gunboat U.S.S. *Michigan*, positioned to guard the prison. Upon landing, the Confederate soldiers had to give over any money they had with them in exchange for notes that they could use to supplement their food rations. Cries of "Fresh fish! Fresh fish!" would ring out as the new men were welcomed and relieved of any property they had managed to keep with them.[i]

Conditions at the prison were appalling. Inside the barracks, pallets were arranged in tiers of three with two men to a bunk. For warmth, there were only straw ticks and thin blankets. Pot-bellied stoves did almost nothing to cut the frigid cold of the Lake Erie winters, and snow blew right through cracks in the barrack walls. Many inmates died from pneumonia and rheumatic fever. Towards the end of the conflict, conditions worsened. Rations were cut so dramatically that the starving prisoners began hunting what they could. One survivor wrote, "We traped [sic] for Rats and the Prisoners Eat Every one they Could get. I taken a mess of Fried Rats. They were all right to a hungry man, was like Fried squirrels."[ii]

Many inmates began planning their escape from Johnson's Island soon after arriving. To escape they would have to overcome daunting obstacles: a 14-foot-high plank fence enclosing the grounds, and inside, a 20-foot invisible boundary called the "dead line" enforced by sentries who were ordered to shoot anyone crossing the line towards the fence. Beyond these barriers were the natural boundaries: the lake, patrolled by the *Michigan*, and in the winter, the ice. The best chance for escape lay in crossing over 30 miles (48km) of frozen lake to Canada in the dead of winter. Not surprisingly, few prisoners even attempted it.

John Bell Steele. Prisoners were society men from the South. After the Civil War, many distinguished themselves as senators, congressmen and judges.

There is only one recorded incident of a successful escape. The night of January 1, 1864, was so cold that the coal-oil lamps lighting the prison grounds froze, and the compound fell dark—it was 26 degrees below zero. The sentries were relieved of their duties for the night, so no one saw five men scale the wall and set out over the ice to Sandusky, three miles (4.8km) away. Nearly frozen to death, two of the men sought shelter in Sandusky where they were surrendered to authorities. The remaining three struck out for Canada. They had no food, and they didn't stop to sleep for more than sixty hours. When they were about a mile from their destination, the ice began to crack, and one man fell through. His fellow escapees managed to rescue him, and the three exhausted men stumbled the rest of the way to Canada. They were free.[iii] Most soldiers, of course, had to wait for the war's end in 1865 before being released. Less fortunate were the 206 men who died on Johnson's Island. They would remain on the island for eternity.

A bizarre incident was said to have occurred on the island some forty years after the Civil War. On a stormy March night, a group of Italian quarrymen took shelter in the prison cemetery. A fierce winter tempest had been punishing the island for three days and

ABOVE & INSET All that is left of the complex is this graveyard, where 206 prisoners were buried.

threatened to blow the quarrymen's shacks away. The men screened themselves from the wind behind a Confederate monument, as icy spray coated the headstones. Then their night turned even more horrifying. One of the workers, Nichola Rocci, recalled looking up at the statue above him and was startled to see that it was moving! It turned around and pointed a flag toward the graves. The dead men responded to the call. Rising from their tombs, ghostly men with hollow eyes, tattered uniforms and muskets slung over their shoulders fell into rank. The stunned workers watched them march through the cemetery and then disappear into the spray. Panic stricken, the quarrymen ran headlong back to their makeshift shacks; as soon as the storm let up, they fled the haunted isle and refused to ever return.

Later quarry workers to Kelleys Island were immigrants from places such as Hungary, Russia, Greece and Italy. The workers lived under the quarry company's thumb; their lodgings were at the quarry, and they spent their pay-cheques in the company-owned store.

# Kelleys Island
# Quarrymen

— ✇ —

Lake Erie was kicking up a powerful storm on the night of June 28, 1899. Off Kelleys Island (near Marblehead, Ohio) the steam freighter *Margaret Olwill* pitched and groaned in the waves, disappearing from sight in each massive trough. All 177 feet (77m) of the steamer shuddered as the bow crested a wave, ran headlong down the backside and then slammed into the next with sickening repetition. The propeller churned in the thrashing lake until the *Olwill's* rudder chains suddenly gave out. The helmsman could do nothing to square the steamer in the waves. As the *Olwill* rolled uncontrollably, cargo lurched back and forth until its weight finally capsized the helpless vessel. The *Olwill* disappeared into the frothing lake, taking down seven crew and two passengers. Only moments later, a nearby ship came to investigate and found no trace of the vessel.[i]

When the lake's anger subsided, the crystal clear water above the *Olwill's* watery grave glittered with renewed innocence. On shore, old-timers recounted the disaster and exchanged suspicions of an accomplice in the sinking of the *Olwill*—the ghosts of Kelleys Island quarrymen.

In 1833 the Kelley brothers, Datus and Irad, bought parcels of land on what was then known as Cunningham Island, or Island No. 6, and began to develop them. Their businesses were varied: winemaking, logging, fruit growing, fishing and quarrying. During the 1840s, the limestone market was booming. In their zeal for profits, the Kelleys ordered their quarrymen to dig further and further, and eventually to tunnel under Lake Erie itself. Some said the tunnel reached almost all the way to the shores of Marblehead on the mainland, a few miles away. [ii] Greed was far outweighing concern for the safety of the company's workers, and on one horrific day, a foreman went too far. He ordered his crew to blast a new stretch of tunnel, even though conditions were dangerous. The men set a charge, and a massive boom rocked the tunnel. Seconds later, water rushed in, trapping and drowning dozens of workers.

For years afterwards, sailors claimed that the ghosts of these men sought revenge on the quarry owners by sinking vessels coming to or leaving the island. The story goes that when ships (especially those carrying stone) passed near Kelleys Island, the ghosts would rise out of their tunnel and drag the ships down.[iii] The *Olwill* was one; the schooner *Young America* was another. In 1880 the schooner, carrying a cargo of stone, foundered in shallow water off Kelleys Island during an August storm. On October 7, 1903, the 141-foot (61-m)

PAGE LEFT In 1833, Datus Kelley and his brother Irad purchased land on Cunningham Island (or Island No. 6) and developed several businesses there. The island now bears their name.

TOP Long after the quarrying disaster, the Kelley Island Lime and Transport Company reached its height in the early 1900s, employing one thousand workers.

RIGHT Later quarry laborers were from so many countries that signs were posted in seven different languages.

LEFT Originally a 108-foot (32.4-m) schooner, the *Adventure* was converted to a propeller steamer in 1897. The wreck now lies 100 feet (30m) from shore in the North Bay of Kelleys Island.

LOWER The steam sandsucker *Sand Merchant* sank in a gale in October of 1936, killing 19 of 26 crewmembers. The vessel now lies inverted in about 60 feet (18m) of water.

Kelleys Island is known for its quantity of limestone and for having the world's longest glacial groove. Only 396 feet (119m) survived the quarry industry.

schooner *Adventure* foundered in a storm in shallow water just offshore in the North Bay of Kelleys Island. And in October 1936, another tragedy. *Sand Merchant*, a steel steam sandsucker used for dredging, succumbed to the pull of the quarrymen. It capsized and sank in an autumn gale, and 19 crewmembers lost their lives.

Now Kelleys Island is primarily a vacation destination, listed on the National Register of Historical Places. Visitors descend every summer to tour the historic neighborhoods (including the Kelley Mansion), view native pictographs and see Glacial Grooves Memorial, the largest example of glacial grooves left in the world. And perhaps tourists to the island encounter other things not mentioned in the brochures—an echo of a quarrying disaster caused by a zeal for profits, and the ghosts of quarrymen seeking revenge for their deaths.

THE FAMOUS BRITISH

# CONVICT SHIP

*THE ONLY ONE LEFT IN THE WORLD*

The CONVICT SHIP "SUCCESS"

**Exhibited at the World's Ports since 1890**

*And Visited by over Fifteen Million People*

THE OLDEST SHIP AFLOAT TO-DAY

Launched at Moulmain, India, 1790, A. D.

The front cover of the pamphlet that accompanied the exhibition of the ship claimed that the *Success* was launched in 1790.

# The Convict Ship
## Success

⁓⁓

In Burma, half a world away from the Great Lakes, a teak barkentine began its varied and worldly career. Its Calcutta owners had the 117-foot (35-m)-long ship built in 1840 for use in the silk trade. By 1849 the *Success* was put to work carrying emigrants to Australia, and two years later it was abandoned at the start of the Australian gold rush. The next owner, in 1852, was the government of Victoria, Australia, who outfitted the barkentine as a prison hulk, lining both decks with cells, and anchoring it off Port Melbourne. It is because of this incarnation that the ship gained the name the Convict Ship *Success*.

The ship was used as a men's prison, a women's prison, a reformatory for boys and an explosives warehouse and was home to some notorious and dangerous criminals. Harry Power (also known as Henry Johnstone) served 14 years on the hulks for shooting a police trooper; and "Mad" Dan Morgan, who served 12 years, is said to have murdered at least four men. Prisoners endured terrible conditions on the hulks, where there was constant violence. There were even two documented murders on board the *Success* prisoners killed warden Owen Owens during an attempted escape, and later Superintendent of Prisons John Price was also killed by prisoners. Public pressure ended the use of the dreaded fleet of prison ships, and most of the hulks were broken up in 1885. While many accounts claim that the *Success* was scuttled and then raised five years later, Richard Norgard, who has been researching the ship, has not found evidence of this and believes it was not.

Alexander Phillips was next in line, buying the *Success* in 1890 for use as a barge. But his employee Edward William Nottingham convinced him of an easier way to profit from the vessel; with so much curiosity surrounding the prison ship, why shouldn't they simply charge admission? They outfitted the *Success* for exhibition—just in time for it to sink at its moorings. Believing the idea could work, a new group refloated the prison hulk and exhibited it at ports around Australia, before it was sailed to London, England, in 1895. By this time rumors were circulating that ghosts haunted the ship: strange apparitions and eerie noises were heard after the visitors had left for the evening. The passage to England took 92 days, and on that voyage, it became clear to the crew that they were not the only souls on board. They reported that arms reached out from the empty prison cells, and terrible moans emanated from vacant cabins.[i] Could it be that the *Success*'s prisoners were still held captive on board?

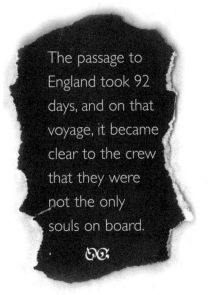

The passage to England took 92 days, and on that voyage, it became clear to the crew that they were not the only souls on board.

At port after port in the British Isles, visitors swarmed to see the ship until 1911, when another group bought and sailed it across the Atlantic to Boston, leaving Liverpool on the same day as the

*Titanic.* American tourists were no different, flocking to see the Convict Ship as it made its way to ports along the Eastern Seaboard. Postcards advertising the exhibit read: "The British Convict Ship, "*Success*" Oldest Ship Afloat, Launched at Moulmein, Burmah 1790." Other advertising promised:

> all the airless dungeons and condemned cells, the whipping posts, manacles, branding irons, punish-ment balls, cat o'nine tails, coffin bath and other fiendish instruments of brutality. She is the oldest ship in the world and the only convict ship left afloat out of that dreadful fleet of ocean Hells which sailed the Seven Seas in 1790. She marked the beginning and end of England's monstrous Penal System. She is unchanged after 135 years, nothing being omitted but the Human Freight.

(It has since been discovered that the *Success* was not sailing in 1790, as it was only built in 1840; and, strictly speaking, the barkentine was not, as was sometimes advertised, part of the "felon fleet" that trans-ported convicts from England to Australia.)

There were more rumors, however, that the *Success*'s "human freight" was not altogether gone. The apparitions that had haunted the crew who sailed the vessel to England reappeared to sailors on the voy-age to the United States. Some of the men saw bizarre ghostly forms prance on the decks, and others refused to go below deck as they heard the screams and moans of the past prisoners.[ii]

From the Eastern Seaboard the *Success* continued its world tour, taking the Panama Canal to the Pacific. It was a feature at the Panama-Pacific Exhibition in San Francisco and then later on in

Seattle before moving on to the Mississippi River system. From here it returned to the Eastern Seaboard and then sailed the Great Lakes. In 1933 the *Success* drew enormous crowds at the Chicago World's Fair. The barkentine toured Great Lakes ports until 1942, when the 102-year-old ship finally retired to a mooring at Sandusky, Ohio, much the worse for wear.

After a heavy storm the following spring, the tired *Success* sank at its moorings (for the second time in its extensive career). But the ship was not allowed to rest. Its last owner, Walter Kolbe, raised it and towed it towards nearby Port Clinton, Ohio. He planned to restore the barkentine and dock it permanently near the Erie Islands. Since shallow water prevented them from sailing into the harbor, Kolbe sailed towards the east side of Port Clinton, where he owned property. But about half a mile from shore, the *Success* ground to a halt in about 18 feet (5.4m) of water and refused to budge. The best Kolbe could do was to salvage some of the teak timbers and other valuables from the sagging hull. Soon after, under the cover of darkness, a thief relieved the Success of a female bust that had graced the bow. Time wore away at the stranded vessel, storms pounded, and winter ice froze and thawed around the hull. Then, on the afternoon of July 4, 1946, as hundreds watched from the shoreline, a magnificent fire blazed, burning the barkentine to the waterline. Most accounts blame vandals for the fire, but there is also speculation that Kolbe himself set the fire because of pressure from the Coast Guard to remove the hazard to navigation.

Of the famous Convict Ship seen by so much of the world, only a few relics remain. Harry Van Stack, who lectured aboard the *Success* from 1925 to 1943, managed to rescue a few articles, including the binnacle (a case for the ship's compass), a teak carving and some old records and photographs, before the ship was turned over to Kolbe. His widow, Louise, donated these items to the Rutherford B. Hayes Presidential Center in Fremont, Ohio, where they are on display. As for the ghosts that haunted the Convict Ship, they seem to have found their final resting place in the waters of Lake Erie and have not been heard from since.

**12. Armour and Headgear,** as worn by Ned Kelly, the notorious Australian highwayman and bushranger. The indents made by well-aimed bullets show what a dangerous fire he was subjected to. He was eventually shot in the arms, legs, and through the face piece; 217 police were on his trail. $10,000 was the reward offered for his capture, dead or alive. The capture of Kelly and his gang cost the Government $600,000.

**13. The Flogging Frames.** With wrists and ankles fastened to the frame, the prisoner was at the mercy of the convict flagellator. The separation of the tails, known as "combing the cats," was insisted upon, twelve strokes with each hand alternately. Men have expired under the lash, their symptoms of distress having been disregarded by the doctor, who was in fault in allowing the flogging to continue. One more hardened than the others after receiving over 100 lashes, and being released, confronted the officials, and offered to "fight the best man among them."

**14 and 15. Original Cat-of-Nine Tails,** made of green hide (untanned leather), bound with brass wire and finished with pellets of lead—Note the initials of the flagellator and other curious markings upon the handle.

The exhibition pamphlet, detailing the gruesome points of being a convict on the ship. The *Success* docked at ports on three continents during its long (1895 to 1942) career as an exhibition ship.

—— ⊗ ——

One Bride's Nightmare

Cries from the Missing Jane Miller

Headless Soldiers

Ghost Horses

# LAKE
# HURON

Between November 15th and November 24th, 1879, the lakes endured a series of incredibly destructive storms. Sixty-five ships met with disaster, including the *Waubuno*.

# One Bride's Nightmare

———————— ⚮ ————————

On November 21, 1879, the steamer *Waubuno* was docked at Collingwood, Ontario, waiting out a November storm on Georgian Bay. Driven by harsh gusts, snow swirled around the vessel as the captain surveyed the black lake for signs that the storm would abate. The steamer was loaded down with cargo and package freight to be delivered up the bay to Parry Sound. With the ice soon closing in and the navigation season coming to an end, communities along Georgian Bay rushed to gather supplies for the long winter ahead. The *Waubuno's* hold was packed to capacity, and the story goes that the captain, despite protesting that the ship was full, was forced to take a ton or two of barreled whiskey on the upper deck. The steamer *Magnetawan*, owned by the rival Georgian Bay Lumber Co., also lay waiting to cast off with a full load of supplies.

Newlyweds Douglass and Elizabeth Doupe watched the ferocious storm as they waited for the captain of the *Waubuno* to give the signal to cast off. They were on their honeymoon and were headed for their new home in the young settlement of McKellar, about 12 miles (19.2km) north of Parry Sound, where Douglass planned on setting up his medical practice. Their furniture, trunks and wedding gifts were

The Collingwood docks were piled with winter supplies destined for communities around Georgian Bay. The Globe Hotel, where *Waubuno* passengers stayed when they left the ship, was located in town to the right.

stowed on an upper deck. "Darling," said the new Mrs. Doupe, "promise not to be angry with me for being a 'fraid-cat, but I had a dreadful dream last night. I dreamt we were on board a steamer somewhere, and then all of a sudden we were not in the steamer at all, but struggling in the water, in the dark, with a lot of people, and something on top of us all, pressing us down." "That was that mince pie we had for supper," replied her husband lightheartedly.

Overhearing the remarks, Captain Burkett reassured Elizabeth that he wouldn't pull out until the snow let up. Still, she suggested to Douglass that they take their possessions off and travel by rail instead. "Now be sensible, dearest. We've bought our tickets, and we'll have to

The *Magnetawan* was still safely docked at Collingwood when the *Waubuno* cast off for the last time.

pay the freight twice over if we do anything so foolish. The Captain is not taking any risks that I can see," replied her husband. Captain Burkett added, "Certainly not with such precious cargo aboard as you, ma'am. We'll just lay here till the snow clears, and we can see our way into the smooth water behind the islands." Another passenger, Noel Fisher, publisher of the *Parry Sound North Star*, piped up, "How long'll that be? If you're going to let O'Donnell beat you with the *Magnetawan*—." Captain Burkett cut him off: "The *Magnetawan*'ll never beat this vessel. [The *Waubuno* is] called after an Indian chief whose name meant Morning Light. He got it because he always showed the way."[i] Fisher joked back that he just wanted to make sure his stock of paper made it to Parry Sound in time for the next week's issue.

Overhearing the remarks, several passengers returned to their hotels in town for the night, confident that the captain would not set out while the storm raged. As they went they reassured one another that they were not doing so because of Mrs. Doupe's fears, only

Erected in 1857, Christian Island Lighthouse was the first official lighthouse to be built on Georgian Bay. Keeper William Hoar may have been the last to see the *Waubuno* before it disappeared.

because the hotel accommodations would be far superior to those on the *Waubuno*. Others stayed on board—ten passengers in all, including the Doupes—to make sure they were there when the captain did cast off. They were familiar with steamboat travel and suspected, given the rivalry between steamship companies, that if the *Magnetawan* set off, Captain Burkett might not wait to fetch the passengers from town. Indeed, at four a.m., the captain signaled the crew to start the paddlewheels churning. Some accounts say that the captain left the bay without so much as a whistle to awaken passengers or to alert the *Magnetawan*. Others claim that he sent the purser to rouse the passengers in town, but they were not willing to leave the warmth of their beds.

In the Doupes' cabin, Elizabeth woke with a start. Outside she could hear the crew preparing to sail. Panicked, she urged her husband to investigate, and they both went out on deck. The ship's boilers were warming up, and the crew was loosening the dock lines. Elizabeth returned to their berth with her husband close behind. "Get the purser, we're leaving," she said as she stuffed clothes into their trunk. Either the steamer pulled away from the dock too quickly for the Doupes to disembark, or Douglass prevented their exit, because the couple was still on board when the *Waubuno* departed Collingwood early that morning.

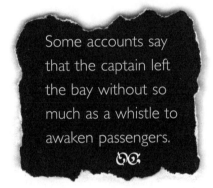

Some accounts say that the captain left the bay without so much as a whistle to awaken passengers.

Sparks flew from the stack as the firemen stuffed the furnace to give the little steamer maximum power in the building waves. Two hours later the *Waubuno* was spotted by the Christian Island lightkeeper, who noted in his logbook that there was a "stiff wind from the nor'west but ship seems to [be] riding well with full cargo." The lightkeeper was perhaps the last to see the cursed steamer that day. When the *Magnetawan* arrived in Parry Sound two days later, its captain was surprised to find a growing heap of cargo on the dock waiting to be shipped. The *Waubuno* had yet to arrive. At first, those on shore thought that Captain Burkett must have anchored in the shelter of an island to wait out the storm, or that he had stopped to find more wood to fuel the steamer. As the hours ticked by, however, alarm grew.

The Parry Sound Lumber Company tug *Mittie Grew* was dispatched to search for the missing vessel. Before long, the searchers found

The *Waubuno*'s engineer, Charlie McQuade, was among those lost. Relatives of the deceased launched lawsuits against the *Waubuno*'s owner, but two successive juries failed to agree on the cause of the disaster.

the obvious signs of a wreck off the islands in the South Channel. Cargo had washed up on the shores, and more floated in the now calmed waves. The search party found a single empty lifeboat and some of the Doupes' furniture. They combed the area for survivors, but by the end of the day, they had only collected the ship's lifebelts, all unused. This led to speculation that the steamer had gone down quickly and without warning.

Stories began to circulate about Elizabeth Doupe's dream. Hadn't the new bride predicted the exact fate of the *Waubuno*? Even the way she had described "something on top of us all, pressing us down" fit with the theories about the wreck that developed over time. Most agree that the *Waubuno* capsized in the giant waves, trapping the passengers and crew below deck. The cargo-laden top deck then ripped away from the hull and floated off into oblivion.

The next spring a man named Pedonquot found the overturned hull of the *Waubuno* in the South Channel behind Moose Point, about four miles (6.4km) southeast of the Haystack Islands. The cause of the wreck, however, remained a mystery until 1959 when three divers solved it. The evidence showed that Captain Burkett probably chugged northward as far as Lone Rock, last of the offshore shoals, before turning eastward into the Waubuno Channel, north of Parry Island. The swirling snowstorm would have hindered visibility,

LEFT  The *Waubuno*'s hull lies just off Wreck Island. LOWER  Haystack Islands.

and it is likely that the captain turned the steamer around and headed towards an opening in the tightly packed islands south of Copperhead. Here, it is argued, he must have come across an uncharted shoal. The natural course of action would have been to drop anchor and wait for calmer seas before navigating around what is now named Burkett Shoal. It is surmised that the anchor hold eventually gave way to the powerful waves, and the windlass was torn from the foredeck. The *Waubuno* was then at the mercy of the shoal, which ground away at the hull and eventually turned the steamer over on the port side, breaking it in two along the main deck, and spilling the cargo, passengers and anything else not attached to the hull into the lake. The passengers and crew never had a chance to escape.

One of the remaining mysteries is where the bodies of the 24 people on board disappeared to, as not one has ever been found. There have also been recent reports of a ghostly presence associated with the wreck. In the late 1980s, a man swimming near Wreck Island (named for the *Waubuno*) supposedly felt the presence of someone or "something" watching him, and he looked up to see a woman in a dark-colored, full-length dress.[ii] Could it have been the tortured spirit of Elizabeth Doupe?

The *Jane Miller* is Georgian Bay's only ghost ship.

# Cries From the Mysterious Jane Miller

— ✸ —

The editor of the *Wiarton Echo* did not attempt to disguise his disgust at what he viewed as the unnecessary wreck of the steamer *Jane Miller* in November 1881:

> It is surmised, and we think correct, that after taking on the extra freight at Meaford, the steamer was top-heavy, and the fact that nearly all, if not all, of her load was on the deck… and there being no ballast, she had simply rolled over without giving a moment's warning. That not one of the victims of the disaster has been found need not be wondered at, when it is considered that the strong gale and snow storm which was raging at the time, no doubt compelled every gangway and other avenue of escape to be clearly closed against the elements without. Thus, completely penned in, and before the slightest effort could be made to save themselves, twenty-eight souls were hurled into eternity without time to utter a prayer.

The *Jane Miller* has never been located.

Certainly the brunt of the blame for the disaster must be shouldered by the master of the top-heavy steamer, *Captain R. D. Port.* The 78-foot (23.4-m) wooden freight and propeller ship *Jane Miller* was reported to be seaworthy, but the captain had the dubious reputation of being daring and foolhardy.

The *Jane Miller* was run by a family operation, as were many smaller coastal steamers—often called "coasters"—on Georgian Bay; the owner was Captain Port's brother, Andrew, and a son, Frank, was the purser. The steamer drew only 7.5 feet (2.25m), making it ideal for servicing the smaller ports where larger ships could not dock. Many of these coasters were fueled by cordwood furnaces, and Georgian Bay was home to several woodcutters who made their living supplying them.

On November 25, 1881, the *Jane Miller* departed Owen Sound, Ontario, with freight and passengers. First stop was Meaford, where the vessel took on more freight and passengers, bringing the total number of passengers and crew to 28. Then the heavily loaded

Main street of Wiarton, c.1900. The *Jane Miller* was heading for Wiarton on the night of November 25, 1881, but it never arrived.

steamer headed west for Wiarton at the end of Colpoy's Bay. A strong southwest gale built on Georgian Bay, and before long, it was punishing the *Jane Miller* with each wave. Battling the mounting storm almost head on, the vessel consumed far more than the usual amount of cordwood. Captain Port made an unscheduled stop at Big Bay to take on more fuel, and at about 8:30 p.m. they pushed off again for Wiarton, about 12 miles (19.2km) further west.

The next day Colpoy's Bay was buzzing over a strange story told by resident Roderick Cameron. The night before, Cameron and his son had been watching the stormy lake from their home along the south shore of Colpoy's Bay. They were expecting a family member who was arriving on the *Wiarton Belle* and were anxious to see the vessel arrive safely. Outside, the snow was driving down in sheets, and the wind was whistling furiously. Just after nine they spotted the lights of a steamer about a half mile (0.8km) from shore heading in the direction of Spencer's Wharf. What happened next puzzled the Camerons. It appeared that the steamer stopped when it was abreast of the wharf, but, just then, blinding snow obliterated their view. When the snow next cleared, the Camerons expected to see a steamer at the wharf, but none was there. And the next day, Cameron learned that no steamer had docked that night to pick up cordwood.

The *Jane Miller* never reached Wiarton. A few days later, patrols were sent out to find out what happened to the vessel. They searched Colpoy's Bay, but found no evidence of a wreck. In an effort to search further, a Wiarton man named McGregor and two others set out from Spencer's Wharf (where the *Jane Miller* regularly stopped for cordwood) towards White Cloud Island. Only a half mile (0.8km) from the wharf they came across large bubbles surfacing on the lake and an obvious discoloration in the water—sure signs of a wreck. They continued on to the island and came across wreckage from the missing steamer: a broken flagstaff, a fire bucket rack, cradles for the lifeboats, a couple of oars painted with the name *Jane Miller*, and five crew caps. This small collection of debris was all that was ever recovered from the steamer.

They came across large bubbles surfacing on the lake and an obvious discoloration in the water.

Colpoy's Bay, 1914. Roderick Cameron and his son believed they saw the *Jane Miller* from their home on Colpoy's Bay on the night it disappeared.

Despite continual dragging of the area, the hull was never found. Its location remains a mystery even today.

There are signs, however, that the souls of the 28 aboard live on at the site of the disaster. On a cold, dark autumn night in the early 1900s, a party of hunters had a frightening experience on White Cloud Island. As they sat around the campfire recounting the day's hunt, cries sprang up from out on the lake—"Help me! God save us!" Peering into the black night, the men couldn't quite decide where the cries were coming from, and it was too dangerous to launch their small boat. A search of the surrounding waters the next morning found nothing. Back on the mainland, when they recounted their experience, the "old salts" in town nodded knowingly. The hunters had heard the ghosts of those lost many years earlier when the *Jane Miller* went down near the island.

TOP At the end of the War of 1812, the British lost Fort Mackinac in the Straits of Mackinac to the Americans. LOWER As replacement, they built Fort Drummond on Drummond Island in 1815.

# Headless Soldiers

West of Manitoulin Island lies a small island with a relatively minor role in Canadian history, but a large one in the ghostly goings on around Lake Huron—Drummond Island. In 1815, near the close of the War of 1812, the British ceded strategic Fort Mackinac on Mackinac Island to the Americans. As replacement, they established Fort Drummond on Drummond Island to continue their trade in furs with the native peoples in the area, and to protect British territory.

With the war over, it almost seemed like the British military authorities forgot about the fort. Official mail could sometimes arrive a full year after being sent. And the fort's Lieutenant Colonel Robert McDouall seemed to be the last to know the British command's intentions. In fact, five months after a truce was called, he was still continuing military actions—his superiors had neglected to inform him of the war's end! Not only was he angry and frustrated himself, but McDouall also had a hard time motivating and disciplining his soldiers. Despite strict rules, the men grew idle and turned to liquor to ease the boredom. Often, provisions never arrived, and in the spring of 1816, five soldiers died of scurvy and many others fell ill. McDouall had finally had enough of this intolerable situation and resigned his post. Subsequent commanders came and went, and British military authorities continually reduced the

ABOVE Lieutenant Colonel Robert McDouall's home at Fort Drummond. McDouall resigned his post in frustration, as his fort was virtually ignored by British command. LEFT Remains of former fireplaces at Fort Drummond.

number of soldiers at the fort. By 1822, the garrison had atrophied to a single company, and conditions were continuing to deteriorate.

John Bigsby, secretary of the British Boundary Commission (set up to survey and determine the exact boundary between the United States and British territory after the War of 1812), documented the soldiers' life at Fort Drummond: "The friendly and intelligent gentlemen of the garrison had little to do save read, hunt for fossils, fish, shoot, cut down trees and plant trees. Their military duties took little of their time." Bigsby wrote a book about the island, *The Shoe and the Canoe*, which told the story of five soldiers who were so fed up with their posting that they slipped away, planning to make their way to the United States and then perhaps home to England. Outraged with this desertion, the commander nailed a reward notice to the barracks door offering twenty dol-

Fort Drummond's abandoned graveyard, 1896.

lars for each soldier—dead or alive. Bigsby relates the story of their capture: Five soldiers started early in the morning across the strait to the American main, and made by the Indian path for Michilimackinac. On arriving there they would be safe. The commandant sent half-a-dozen Indians after them, who in a couple of days returned with the men's heads in a bag. The Indians knew of a short cut and got ahead of their prey and lay in ambush behind a rock in the track. When the soldiers came within a few feet the Indians fired, and in the end killed every one of them.

A differing account tells of two Indian runners on snowshoes who surprised the men as they dozed by a fire on a Manitoulin Island beach. They chopped off their heads with tomahawks, then carried the heads back to the fort as proof. In his book *Drummond Island, the Story of the British Occupation 1815–1828*, Samuel F. Cook writes that the headless trunks of these men "remained sitting on the log and warming themselves by the fire which made the night lurid with its glare. And ever since, unburied, they wander on those shores, seeking the heads which there they lost while sleeping." For some, the torment of life at Fort Drummond finally ended; for these unfortunates, it never did.

The wreck of the *Alice Hackett* near Fitzwilliam Island was Georgian Bay's first shipwreck.

# Ghost Horse
# From the Alice Hackett

Headless soldiers are not the only ghosts associated with the ill-fated Fort Drummond. It took six years after the close of the War of 1812 to determine an exact boundary between the United States and British territory, and so it was not until 1822 that the British soldiers at Fort Drummond received notification that Drummond Island had been awarded to the Americans. A full six years after that, in November 1828, two ships, the brig *Duke of Wellington* and the smaller American schooner *Alice Hackett*, arrived to relocate the small community to Penetanguishene, on southern Georgian Bay.

In all, 91 people were aboard the two ships, including officers and soldiers, their families, servants and settlers from the area around the fort. The larger *Duke of Wellington* took most of the supplies and soldiers, and the Alice Hackett picked up the remaining soldiers as well as the civilians, including a tavern keeper named Fraser. Soon after they set out, the weather turned bad, and by evening, a full-scale autumn gale was charging across Lake Huron. *The Duke of Wellington* managed to make it through and arrived safely in Penetanguishene. The *Alice Hackett*, however, was battling more than just the storm.

In the *Sudbury Star*, Rev. H.J.L. Wooley of Richards Landing described the *Alice Hackett*'s voyage:

The good ship had weathered many a rough gale on the lakes and would doubtless have delivered her cargo and crew safely at the post on Georgian Bay had not the fort tavern-keeper taken on board that morning thirteen barrels of whiskey besides other odd bits of liquid dynamite. He was a wily merchant, used to trading with all manner of men, and knew the power of a few free drinks to enhance big business in his line. No sooner had Drummond Island faded into the blue haze and windy cloud sheets on the western horizon, than he tapped a barrel and called all hands to drink a last toast to "Awld Drummond."

Those on board were eager for the distraction, and passengers and crew fell into varying states of inebriation.

By nighttime, thunderous waves were assaulting the schooner, but no one appears to have been paying much attention. Indeed, around midnight, when the schooner lurched to a halt with a huge crash, someone shouted out "Yo! Ho! In port at last," and a cheer went up. Far from the safety of port, the *Alice Hackett* was stranded on some

At the end of the War of 1812, the British lost this strategic fort in the Straits of Mackinac to the Americans. As replacement, they built Fort Drummond on Drummond Island in 1815.

rocks off Fitzwilliam Island, southeast of Manitoulin Island. The crew managed to launch the yawl, and it was rowed to the island along with the remainder of the whiskey. The men gathered close together and, owing to the whiskey, "were soon oblivious to the world's mad strife."

The next morning they were roused by a panicked cry from a man named Pierre Lapine, who realized that in their drunken rush towards the safety of shore the men had left behind the only woman on board and her young daughter—Pierre's wife and child! The men launched the yawl and made their way back to the wreck of the *Alice Hackett* to find Angelina and the girl, cold and hungry, but still alive. The resourceful woman had tied her child and herself to the mast, where they were able to survive the wild night.

Three days later, soldiers from Penetang rescued the stranded passengers, but they had to leave one soul on the island—a white saddle horse named Louie. Louie was the pride and joy of William Solomon, who had farmed on Drummond Island and had worked as an interpreter. Solomon was crushed at the prospect of leaving his fine carriage horse behind, but there was not enough room for Louie on

Antoine Labatte's father was a soldier stationed at Drummond for eleven years. The *Alice Hackett* was towing a bateau with the Labatte family of six and others when the wreck occurred. Captain Hackett, who had previously been in a ship fire, and had been rescued clinging to wreckage, made a strong impression on Antoine, even though he was only three years old at the time of the incident. Antoine recalled, "Captain Hackett was badly burned on one side of his face and neck, so that the cords were drawn down, causing a peculiar twitching of the muscles and a continual turning of his face to one side."

the ship. Throwing his arms around the horse's neck, he promised to return for him. Louie just snorted back with indifference. With the run of Fitzwilliam to himself, he lived out his days in a virtual horse paradise. Solomon made repeated attempts to convince fish boat masters and fur traders to retrieve his prized animal, but in vain. Fitzwilliam became known as Horse Island to those who knew it. Long after Louie's death, sailors would speak of seeing the ghost of the white horse galloping up and down the shore while they sailed past on dark autumn nights. Those aboard the *Alice Hackett* that dreadful night were fortunate to have survived. With any less luck, it

could be they who continue to roam Horse Island's shores for eternity.

Fitzwilliam Island is still called Horse Island by Georgian Bay fishermen. The Fitzwilliam fishing station (seen here) has long been abandoned.

Four elderly voyageurs, photographed in Penetanguishene in 1895. Lewis Solomon (far left) was born on Drummond Island in 1821 and was five years old when the *Alice Hackett* wrecked. He recalled the incident with some sarcasm, "The passengers, crew and captain, in a somewhat advanced stage of drunkenness, managed to reach the shore in safety; also one horse [his father's], some pork, and 13 barrels of whiskey, though the whole company were much too intoxicated to entertain an intelligent idea of the operation, but were sufficiently conscious of what they were doing to secure the entire contingent of whiskey." About the abandoned mother and child, he was quoted as saying, "Mrs. Lepine[sic], in the darkness and fury of the storm, wrapped the babe in a blanket, and having tied it on her back, lashed herself securely to the mast, and there clung all night long through a furious storm of wind and drenching rain, from eleven o'clock till daylight, or about six o'clock in the morning, when the maudlin crew, having recovered in a measure from their drunken stupor, rescued her." The *Alice Hackett* and remaining cargo were a total loss. The pummeling waves caused a cannon on board to fall down the hatch and through the hull.

---⊗⊗---

The Lake's First Ghost Ship—Le Griffon

A Sailor's Hunch

She Has Gone to Pieces

Fort Dearborn Massacre

# LAKE
# MICHIGAN

ABOVE The *Griffon* was the first ship to sail on the Great Lakes above Niagara Falls. RIGHT INSET La Salle was notorious for his inability to keep crew. He worked his men so hard and paid them so infrequently that there are reports of at least sixty desertions.

# The Lake's First Ghost Ship
## —Le Griffon

The story of the *Griffon* may be the most fabled of all Great Lakes ghost stories. Notorious French explorer René-Robert Cavelier Sieur de la Salle launched the 60-foot (18-m) barque in 1679, a monumental craft for a time when most Great Lakes travel was by canoe. The first commercial vessel on the Lakes, it was also the first to "sail through a crack in the Lake." And over 300 years after the barque disappeared on Lake Michigan, it remains one of the most sought after and debated vessels amongst wreck enthusiasts.

La Salle had convinced France's King Louis XIV to sanction his plan to explore the Mississippi River to its mouth, and to set up fur-trading forts along the route. For this, he needed a suitable barque on the upper Great Lakes, but there was the small obstacle of Niagara Falls. He and his crew sailed up the St. Lawrence River, across Lake Ontario and up the

ABOVE  Friar Louis Hennepin and Henry De Tonty supervised the building of the *Griffon*. La Salle spent much of this time at Fort Frontenac dealing with his troubled affairs. RIGHT  Friar Louis Hennepin's drawing of Niagara Falls. Most of what we know of the *Griffon*'s ill-fated voyage has been gleaned from Hennepin's writing and drawings.

Niagara River, landing at the present site of Lewiston, New York. Here the men shouldered the building materials up the Niagara Escarpment and around Niagara Falls. They established their shipyard near the mouth of the Cayuga Creek, which empties into the Niagara River, and built the now famous *Griffon*. The vessel was named in honor of the French governor, the Comte de Frontenac, whose coat of arms bore the griffin, a mythical creature with a lion's body and the head and wings of an eagle. As the barque slid into the water for the first time, La Salle is said to have cried out, "High above the black crows shall the gallant *Griffon* soar."[i]

In August 1679 the new barque set sail on its first long voyage, bound for Green Bay on Lake Michigan. The 32 men aboard have been described as "saints and sinners, scoundrels and scholars, soldiers of fortune, Franciscan friars, schemers and brandy traders."[ii] Perhaps the most interesting crewmember was the pilot, sometimes referred to as "Luke the Dane." By all accounts he was a massive man, seven feet tall and imposing in manner. He was known to be violent with the crew and spoke out of turn when dealing with superiors. Despite his ill temper, Luke was a good pilot, and considering that he and the crew were owed a year's back pay, perhaps some hostility was understandable. (La Salle was well known for his inability to keep crew. There are accounts of resentful crewmembers trying to poison him; in fact, La Salle met his end at the hand of one of his own men who shot him in the back of the head.)

There was a near disaster even before the ship left Lake Erie. The voyage's chronicler, Friar Louis Hennepin, wrote that while sailing in a thick fog, La Salle heard breaking water. He turned the barque away from the dreaded noise, but despite taking continual soundings, the crew could not find the lake bottom. Of course, at the time there was scant information available about navigational hazards on the lake. La Salle had viewed a rough sketch of Long Point made in 1669 by René Brehant de Galinée (a Sulpician priest who took detailed notes

LEFT Friar Louis Hennepin was the ship's spiritual counselor and chronicler. RIGHT One of Friar Louis Hennepin's drawings, believed to depict La Salle and Hennepin himself.

on the geography of the Lakes), but he did not know where the point was. Eventually the fog burned off, revealing the dangerous sand cape... straight in front of him.

La Salle sailed Lake Huron, made a brief stop at Michilimackinac, and then negotiated his way through the jumble of islands in upper Lake Michigan before arriving safely in Green Bay. Here, his first task was to load the *Griffon* with beaver pelts. With the cost of building the *Griffon* and launching the voyage, La Salle was in terrible financial condition, and his creditors were impatiently awaiting payment at Niagara. La Salle gave orders for Luke and five crewmembers to sail back to Niagara with the pelts as quickly as possible. They were to return with materials to build another vessel, this one for La Salle's planned exploration of the Mississippi River. Expecting that Luke and the *Griffon* would soon return, La Salle headed for the area now known as Peoria, Illinois, where he intended to build the next ship.

Hennepin wrote that the barque left Green Bay on September 18th in a westerly wind with Luke and five crewmembers aboard. After that, there are varying theories, the only certainty being that the *Griffon* disappeared soon after it left Green Bay. The theory La Salle believed is that Luke led the crew in stealing the pelts, selling them, and then scuttling the *Griffon* to hide the evidence. Others blamed the native

Potawatomi or the Ottawa, fur traders, and even Jesuits for the disappearance. Of course, it is possible that the *Griffon* foundered in a storm, although this theory lacks the intrigue of the others!

Following the disappearance, La Salle gradually gathered reports of his lost ship. A year after the *Griffon* sailed over the horizon, he met a group of Potawatomi who had seen the *Griffon* anchored in a bay in northern Lake Michigan two days after the departure from Green Bay. Two years after this, La Salle met another native man who told him about five white men who were making their way down the Mississippi in canoes full of goods when they were captured by other natives along the river. Four of the men were killed. One, who fit the distinctive description of Luke the Dane, was spared. La Salle supposed that Luke was trying to reach French explorer Daniel Greysolon, also known as Sieur du Lhut, in order to trade the furs that had filled the hold of the *Griffon.*

As much or more mystery surrounds the location of the wreck. Many have claimed to have found the famous vessel, but two

This drawing of the *Griffon* shows the bow bearing a figure of a griffin, a mythical animal with the body and legs of a lion and the back and wings of an eagle.

wrecks stand out as being the most credible: one lies near Russell Island (formerly Rabbit Island) off the tip of Lake Huron's Bruce Peninsula and the other on the western end of Manitoulin Island, also on Lake Huron. The wreck off Russell Island was still in decent condition when Orrie Vail of Tobermory showed it to some experts in 1955. Its size and shape matched the description of the *Griffon*, and hand-hammered bolts appeared to be evidence that the wreck was old enough to be the *Griffon*.

The Manitoulin site offers even more mystery. Manitoulin residents have long recalled stories about a wreck located on a rocky

The Mississagi Strait lighthouse is now a museum.

beach on the western tip of the island. Early settlers pillaged the wreck for its iron bolts and lead caulking. When experts were able to examine what remained, the wood samples, the ship's design and the caulking matched a ship of the *Griffon*'s era.[iii] The wreck has since slipped back into the depths, but there is another part of the story that gives one pause. Shortly before the end of the nineteenth century, Mississagi Strait lightkeeper William Cullis and his assistant, John Holdsworth, made a grisly discovery. They were combing the shoreline in search of a tree for a new boat spar when they scared up a white rabbit, which promptly dove out of sight. Curious, Holdsworth followed its trail and, pulling earth and foliage away, soon discovered the

The *Griffon*. La Salle believed that his pilot, Luke, had led the crew in selling La Salle's pelts to traders and then scuttled the ship to hide the evidence.

entrance to a large cave. Inside was a stunning discovery— the skeletons of six men. Scattered nearby were some buttons and other trinkets. The skulls were kept by local residents and have since been lost, but one was decidedly that of an unusually large man who could have been Luke the Dane. One Manitoulin Islander remembers the antics of Jim Doyle, another resident, who was able to put the entire jawbone over his own jaw.

In the 1960s, articles were written buoying the legitimacy of one wreck over the other, but wherever the bones of the *Griffon* may lie, the ghost of the vessel is said to still haunt the lakes. Old-timers have reported seeing the barque "coasting along the north end of Lake Michigan, with all sails set."[iv] The tiny barque may still be trying to deliver its cargo of furs for La Salle, despite being cut down early in its career, perhaps by its own crew.

A hand-threaded iron bar with nut and washer was sent to Paris, France, for analysis at the *Laboratoire d'essais du Conservatoire national des arts et métiers*. The report stated, "the threaded bar which we have been studying represents all characteristics of antiquity for a piece of iron manufactured by a process used in France before the 18th century. In particular it could have been manufactured some time before 1679 when the *Griffon* disappeared."

Captain Henry Kelley had the schooner *Our Son* built in 1875. It survived to be among the last of the Great Lakes sailing ships, a remnant of a time when nearly 2,000 schooners sailed the Lakes.

# A Sailor's Hunch

In 1875 Captain Kelley, a prosperous Great Lakes shipmaster, commissioned the building of a second schooner to double his shipping operations. Construction took place in Kelley's home port of Lorain, Ohio, on the Black River. All was going well when tragedy struck. One day, Kelley's first child, Harry, was playing near the ship when he fell into the river and drowned. Captain Kelley stalwartly continued with preparations for the launch. As the new 185-foot (55.5-m) schooner splashed into the Black River, he revealed the freshly painted name on the stern—*Our Son*. The schooner had three tall masts to carry 16 sails. "The finest monument any sailor ever had. Harry would be proud," remarked Kelley to his grieving wife.[i] Capable of sailing at a speed of up to 15 knots and carrying 1,000 tons of ore or 40,000 bushels of grain, the schooner served Kelley well. Nonetheless, Kelley sold it in 1879, and, over the years, *Our Son* went on to have several owners.

By the 1890s, the once proud schooner was quite changed from its original state, relegated to use as a barge towed behind the newer, faster steam-powered *J. H. Outhwaite*. The three masts were cut short, and the 60-foot (18-m) nose pole was gone. Fortunately, in

In the 1890s, *Our Son* was relegated to use as a barge, towed behind
the steamer *J. H. Outhwaite*.

1923 *Our Son* fell into more sympathetic hands. Captain Nelson, one of the last of the "schooner men," with over fifty years' experience sailing the Lakes, bought the vessel and gave it renewed life. He had a contract to carry spruce and balsam timbers from Georgian Bay on Lake Huron to the Muskegon Paper Company's plant on Lake Michigan. Nelson outfitted the stubby masts with six sails so that the schooner might resume shipping under its own power. Despite his improvements, there was a noticeable dampness below deck, and the fore and aft ends were dropping badly. The hull bore the scars of numerous impacts with canal locks and wharves, each mark a sign of the vessel's age like the growth rings on the timbers *Our Son* hauled.

In September 1930, Lake Michigan took a run at the old schooner. On the evening of the 25th, Captain Nelson and his crew of six were sailing towards Muskegon, Michigan, with a hold full of timbers. They were making good time in a strong westerly wind. The next day, however, the westerly built to near hurricane velocity. Before they could reach shelter, *Our Son* became waterlogged and almost impossible to control. The sails blew apart from the strain, leaving the schooner at the mercy of waves that reached thirty feet (9m) above the bulwarks. Nelson struggled at the helm, as his crew hoisted the American flag upside down to signal their distress to other vessels, even though, having been blown so far out of the shipping lanes, the possibility of encountering another vessel was slim. Waves crashed on the deck, and water threatened to flood into the hatches. Rope, boxes and barrels roamed the deck, shifting with every roll and pitch.

"There's water in the hold, lots of it," reported one of the crew. Although *Our Son* was carrying a yawl, Nelson considered it riskier to launch it in the swirling waves than to stay on the battered schooner. They would have to wait out the storm and hope that the schooner held together. With no radio on board, they could not send out a distress signal, but Nelson was sending out a different type of signal that day—he was praying to God that someone would find them.

Far to the northwest, the steamer *William Nelson* was downbound with a cargo of sand destined for South Chicago. The *William Nelson* had hit the storm head on at dawn after passing through the Straits of Mackinac. Captain Charles H. Mohr surveyed the boiling lake and made a plan to minimize the danger; he would stay close to Lansing Shoal, then hug the north shore of Summer Island and St. Martin Island, and finally anchor to the lee of Washington Island until the gale blew itself out. What happened next, however, was not part of his plan. By some inexplicable force, Mohr was drawn to the east shore of Lake Michigan and found himself, against all rules of seamanship, ordering a course for the dangerous Manitou Passage. As the waves built, pounding the *William Nelson* broadside, the crew must have been shocked and confused at the decision. Each wave wreaked more damage on the steamer; dishes crashed from galley shelves, glass portholes were smashed in, secured watertight doors were thrust open, and even bulkheads were bent in. Why was Captain Mohr putting his vessel and crew in such a precarious position?

That same afternoon, safe on dry land on the lake's eastern shore stood another piece to the strange puzzle that is *Our Son*. One of Captain Mohr's old friends, Joseph A. Sadony, was with a small group, watching the waves hurl against the beach with tremendous force. Gazing out over the angry lake, they wondered if any vessels were caught in the gale. Sadony spoke up: "There is one sailing ship to the northwest I would not want to be on." Another commented that surely there weren't still sail-powered vessels working the Great Lakes shipping lanes. But Sadony went on to describe a vision he had of a schooner—the hold filling with water, the sails in tatters and the rigging in a tangled mess. The astonished group listened as Sadony elaborated. The vessel was far off the shipping lanes, but he could feel the presence of another ship, which would come across the schooner—if its captain continued to follow his intuition.

By some inexplicable force, Mohr was drawn to the east shore of Lake Michigan and found himself, against all rules of seamanship, ordering a course for the dangerous Manitou Passage.

Back on the *William Nelson*, Mohr was navigating the treacherous eastern shore. Just south of Ludington, Michigan, he turned hard to starboard and headed west towards the distant Wisconsin shore, directly into the massive waves. As for *Our Son*, the schooner was still afloat, but daylight and hope were beginning to fade. The fo'c'sle deck was collapsing inward, bending the stanchions and beams, and the pilothouse window was broken. Each wave that hit threatened to take the schooner down.

It was then that the *William Nelson* came across the helpless vessel. Still, the danger was not over, as the heavy seas made it impossible for the steamer to launch a lifeboat. Mohr began by sending out an S.O.S.—if the rescue did not go perfectly, there was a good chance his own vessel would need assistance. When Mohr could see the smoke from the stack of the *Pere Marquette Car Ferry No. 22*, he circled *Our Son* and spread a film of oil over the water to calm the crests of the breaking waves. Next, he prepared to bring his bow to the schooner, a maneuver that ran the risk of causing the ships to collide and possibly sink. Anticipating the *William Nelson's* next move, Captain Nelson and the crew of *Our Son* lined up on the port side. Sounds of cracking and straining wood filled the air as the steamer's bow came in contact with the sagging schooner. The crew leapt onto the *William Nelson*, and the steamer backed away quickly, its engine straining hard.

In the pilothouse of the *William Nelson*, Captain Nelson described their ordeal: "The waves were thirty, forty... yes, and some fifty feet high. But still Tom Larsen [the cook] wouldn't come out of the galley until I told him a ship was coming to save us."[ii] Captain Mohr turned the *William Nelson* towards safety, and finally, at 5:30 p.m. on the 27th, the steamer docked at South Chicago. Word of the rescue had already spread, and the press was waiting at the docks. In an interview, Nelson gave an eerie depiction of the experience on *Our Son*: "There would be times of silence when we were down in the deep troughs between the seas. The crests would be high above us on either side and the wind would be whistling over them. But down where we were, it was awful quiet at times." He expressed his extreme gratitude for Mohr's rescue, calling it "a magnificent feat... the kind only a superb shipmaster like Captain Mohr could carry out."[iii] Mohr's bravery was rewarded with a congressional medal by the American government for what was deemed to be "one of the most daring pieces of expert seamanship in the history of navigation." [iv]

Sometime later, the old friends Mohr and Sadony were able to compare notes about their strange experiences on that 26th of September. Sadony was known amongst his acquaintances for an ability to divine what was happening in far-off places and sometimes to predict the future. Sadony told Mohr of the visions he had had of the schooner, and Mohr recounted the powerful force of intuition that brought him to the rescue of *Our Son*. Long before this event, the two friends had spoken about hunches and had agreed that they would both follow the pull of their instincts. Perhaps because of their agreement, the two men were able to hear *Our Son* as it cried out in the storm.

According to one report, the ship's dog was found wandering on the beach near St. Joseph, Michigan, a few days after the *Chicora*'s accident.

# She Has Gone
## to Pieces

—————————————— ⟪⟫ ——————

In the late 1800s the steamer *Chicora* was considered one of the best
on the Great Lakes. Not only was it appointed with exceptional staterooms and paneled with rich mahogany and cherry woods, but it also
had a "guaranteed speed of seventeen miles per hour!"[i] Launched in
Detroit in 1852, the 217-foot (65.1-m) wood passenger and package
freight steamer made regular trips across lower Lake Michigan
between Milwaukee, Wisconsin, and St. Joseph, Michigan.

In the late fall of 1894, the *Chicora* was put into winter stor-
age at St. Joseph after a busy navigation season. The risks to shipping
from storms and ice were too great to warrant extending the season.
That January, however, unusual circumstances brought the *Chicora* out
of its customary winter rest. There had been a late grain harvest, and
surplus flour being stored in Milwaukee needed to reach market. In
order to be loaded on boxcars and distributed, it first had to be
shipped to St. Joseph. Making the return trip across Lake Michigan
was a gamble, but the president of Graham and Morton
Transportation Company, John H. Graham, wagered it would be possible to do two or even three runs if the weather held.

The *Chicora* passing through the Sault Ste. Marie locks. When it went missing, the *Chicora* was loaded down with 640 tons of flour, enough to fill 40 railcars.

Captain Edward Stines was chosen for the trip. He had worked for Graham and Morton for 25 years and was considered very competent. Some crew spaces had to be filled with new recruits, since many of the crewmembers had found other employment over the winter. The captain's 23-year-old son, Benjamin, was hired as a temporary second mate. James R. Clark acted as a replacement clerk, and he brought along, as a passenger, a friend named Joseph Pearl.

On the otherwise uneventful trip from St. Joseph over to Milwaukee where the flour was to be loaded, Pearl managed to infuriate Captain Stines. Out on the lake, a duck had alighted on the *Chicora*—a strange sight so far from shore and in mid-winter. The captain was horrified as he watched Pearl take aim and shoot the bird dead. His sense that the shot bird was an evil omen filled Stines with such dread that he could not contain it. His fear spread through the crew, and when the

On that dreadful day, the president of Graham and Morton managed to stop another of his ships, the *Petoskey*, from sailing.

boat was being loaded in Milwaukee, the captain even mentioned the bad omen to others on the dock.

At four a.m. on January 21, 1895, owner John Graham surveyed the barometer in his St. Joseph home. It registered 28, the lowest he had ever seen, and the *Chicora* was scheduled to sail back from Milwaukee that morning! Graham raced down to the dock in time to stop his other ship, the *Petoskey*, from casting off. Then he ordered the telegraph operator to send an urgent message to the *Chicora*. As soon as the telegram was received, a bike courier was dispatched. The courier arrived at the docks at five a.m. to find the *Chicora* just pulling away. No one could hear his shouts of "telegram for Captain Stines" above the din of the boilers and churning propeller.

Most likely, Captain Stines also saw the barometer that morning, but what the instrument could not predict was the time that the storm would arrive. Perhaps Stines gambled that the *Chicora* would make the seven-and-a-half-hour trip before the storm struck? An hour after casting off, however, the *Chicora* ran into appalling conditions. A ferocious winter storm was sweeping across Lake Michigan. By nine

The *Chicora* was bound for St. Joseph, Michigan, when it went missing.

a.m., the gusts reached hurricane force, and snow and ice were accumulating on the decks.

When the vessel did not arrive in St. Joseph at the expected time, the alarm was sounded. Graham sent telegrams to ports along the route, hoping to hear that the *Chicora* had taken refuge from the storm. All replies came back negative. His worst fears were confirmed when wreckage began to wash ashore. On January 24th, a telegram from South Haven, Michigan (about 35 miles [56km] north of St. Joseph), came in: "port side and forward upper bulwarks five feet wide and twelve feet long, and inside shutters to passenger gangway all belonging to the *Chicora*, were found this morning about a mile out on the ice."[ii]

The tug *Crosby* and two steamers, the *Petoskey* and *Nyack*, joined a search for any crewmembers who may have survived on floating ice. The teams turned up curtains, decorations, cargo, planking and two spars, but no survivors. In fact, no bodies were ever found (although reports mention that the ship's dog was found alive on the beach near St. Joseph a few days after the disaster).

Some observers on shore claimed to have witnessed the *Chicora* give its last gasp before succumbing to the torrent. Seventeen-year-old Henry Gross reported hearing a ship's whistle blowing repeatedly at a

The steamer *Nyack* joined the *Petoskey* and tug *Crosby* in the search for survivors.

point seven miles (11.2km) below South Haven. Could this have been the *Chicora* calling for help? Several South Haven residents described seeing the lights of a vessel, which then disappeared. William Hare also reported seeing the doomed freighter near South Haven: "Her stern was down and she appeared to be sinking. There were no spars and I saw no signs of life nor did I hear any disaster signals." [iii]

But the closest anyone came to understanding the chilling tale of the last hours on the doomed *Chicora* came from two notes that were recovered, floating in bottles. The first read "All is lost. Could see land if not snowed and blowed. Engines give out, drifting to shore in ice. Captain and clerk swept off. We have a hard time of it. 10:15 o'clock." Another read, "*Chicora* engines broke. Drifted into trough of sea. We have lost all hope. She has gone to pieces. Good bye, McClure, Engineer." [iv]

Should blame for the accident fall on the owner of the *Chicora*, John Graham, who gambled with the winter weather on Lake Michigan, or was there more to the calamity than atrocious weather? Perhaps the dread that the captain felt after the needless shooting of the duck was well founded. Could his premonition have been real?

ABOVE Fort Dearborn. PAGE RIGHT Fort Dearborn was named after Henry Dearborn, a hero during the American Revolution.

# Fort Dearborn Massacre

———  ☙❧  ———

Buried deep in the annals of Chicago history is the story of a massacre near Fort Dearborn and rumors of ghosts that haunt the terrible site. The American government built the fort in 1803 to protect the strategic region at the mouth of the Chicago River, which offered access to hunting and fishing grounds, agricultural land and important trade routes. By the summer of 1812, Fort Dearborn was teeming with activity. In the words of one observer, Nelson Algren, the population at the fort in 1812 was a mix of "Yankee and voyageur, the Irish and the Dutch, Indian traders and Indian agents, half breed and quarter breed and no breed at all."[i] Whereas this vast, wild land had once provided enough for everyone, problems had begun to surface. Tension was mounting between the different groups. There was increased competition for trading routes and hunting areas, and the once self-sufficient Potawatomi Indian population had become dependent on trade goods.

By 1800, there was increased competition for hunting areas and trade routes. Native groups in the area became more reliant on trade goods for survival.

The climate lent itself to traders and entrepreneurs. One such man was John Kinzie, who arrived in the area around 1803 and immediately set the tone of his negotiating style. Kinzie purchased land on the shore of the Chicago River from a Pierre Menard, who claimed that he had bought it from an Indian named Bonhomme. The problem was that another man, John Lalime, also laid claim to the same parcel of land. Lalime had bought it from Jean Baptiste DuSable, who had lived at the river's edge for about twenty years and is noted by many historians as Chicago's first settler. Kinzie chose to end the rivalry by murdering Lalime.

Until 1812, Kinzie was *the* trader at Fort Dearborn. Later, in her book *Wau-Bun: The "Early Day" in the North-West,* Juliette M. Kinzie wrote glowingly of the father-in-law she never met. By her account, Kinzie was a "courtly" gentleman, friend to the Indians and a leader. In reality, he was a hard-drinking, brawling opportunist who had a stranglehold on the fur trade at the fort. His sense of superiority over his French Creole and native neighbors and his way of doing business affected the attitudes of other settlers at Fort Dearborn, where theft,

ABOVE In 1804, forty-year-old John Kinzie arrived to establish a trading post near the newly constructed Fort Dearborn. Kinzie ruled trade at the fort until 1812, when the fort was abandoned. He returned in 1816, but the stronger American Fur Company had already moved in.

slander and even murder reigned. Not surprisingly, the group's treatment of the Potawatomi eventually caused resentment.

In 1812, Kinzie's empire disintegrated when fighting erupted along the northwest frontier between the Americans and the British. About a month after war was declared, General William Hull, the commander of the North West Army for the Americas, ordered the evacuation of Fort Dearborn. On site, Captain Nathan Heald ordered all the fort's whiskey and gunpowder destroyed and then led a group of about 148 soldiers and settlers across the open plains towards the safety of Fort Wayne, Indiana. A group of Potawatomi, who were allied with the British, was secretly watching the progress of this band. As the soldiers and settlers reached what is today 16$^{th}$ Street and Indiana Avenue, the Potawatomi ambushed. They overwhelmed the soldiers, killing the ensign and the surgeon's mate, and badly wounding Captain Heald. When the Potawatomi weapons were finally lowered, 86 adults and 12 children lay dead or dying. In the distance, the fort was engulfed in flames. The settlers and soldiers surrendered. Potawatomi Chief Blackbird accepted Heald's desperate offer of one hundred dollars for every man still alive. One of the survivors described being struck with horror at:

> the sight of men, women and children lying naked,
> with principally all their head off, and passing over
> the bodies I was confident I saw my wife with her

ABOVE  In 1812 fighting erupted along the northwest frontier and General Hull ordered the evacuation of Fort Dearborn. PAGE LEFT  Mrs. Rebekah Heald, wife of Captain Nathan Heald who led the soldiers and settlers of Fort Dearborn away from the fort and into an ambush.

head off, about two feet from her shoulders; tears for the first time rushed to my eyes but I consoled myself with [the] firm belief that I should soon follow her.[ii]

Using his wiles, Kinzie managed to negotiate the release of his family and himself, but others were not so fortunate. The attackers enslaved those who had survived the ordeal and eventually sold many of them to the British, whereupon they finally regained their freedom. The dead remained where they fell, and it was not until four years later that American troops re-entered the area and found the disturbing scene.

There are rumors that the Fort Dearborn site is protected by the ghostly figures of troops who show the scars of battle.[iii] However, the actual site of the massacre lay dormant, its horrors forgotten…

George Pullman had Pullman City built for his workers. The town included state-of-the-art housing, a church, a library, landscaped parks and Athletic Island, and a five-acre sports facility.

until years later when the city of Chicago had expanded as far as the site. When road workers began digging up remains dating from the time of the massacre, people in the area reported strange appearances of what they termed "settlers."[iv] Were the spirits of the slain beginning to appear?

In the 1890s, the socially progressive George Pullman, inventor of the Pullman sleeper railcar, built a model city for his workers right on the site of the massacre. He believed that his employees should enjoy good housing set in a beautiful landscape, should be well paid, and should be given opportunities for culture and recreation. Pullman City offered this, and in 1893 it was celebrated as proof that a corporation could improve the quality of life of its workers, a major issue of the day. Pullman did not ignore the history of the site; in fact, he commissioned a bronze statue to commemorate the Fort Dearborn Massacre. It was dedicated before a group of Chicago notables in 1893.

Unfortunately, Pullman's utopian city was short-lived. In 1894 the company was losing money, and Pullman cut his workers' wages by 25 per cent. A delegation of employees met with him to

request that he lower the living costs in the town (rent, groceries, etc.) to offset the wage cuts. Not only did Pullman refuse, but he also fired the men the next day—an ill-considered action that prompted a nasty strike. Events escalated when the American Railway Union aided the workers in their cause by refusing to deal with any train that used Pullman cars. President Grover Cleveland even sent in federal troops to break the strike and to ensure that the mail on the trains was delivered. All of Pullman's employees were forced to sign a statement promising that they would never join a union. Pullman's reputation was in ruin, and it was further damaged when a presidential commission investigated the incident. About Pullman City, the report had this to say: "The aesthetic features are admired by visitors, but have little money value to employees, especially when they lack bread." The State of Illinois filed suit against Pullman and took back ownership of the town, which was amalgamated into the city of Chicago. By the time Pullman died in 1897, he was so hated by his employees that his family was frightened his body would be stolen and held hostage for ransom.

For the second time in less than one hundred years, a community was destroyed, arguably because its leaders did not respond to the needs of the citizens. At Fort Dearborn, Kinzie and his friends were not respectful of the Potawatomi, and when power shifted, the Potawatomi took revenge. In Pullman City, Pullman appeared to forget about his utopian dream when a depression hit and his employees turned on him. A journalist who was covering the dedication of the bronze statue, which Pullman erected at the Fort Dearborn Massacre site, connected these two incidents:

> Me thinks this place is haunted and a subtle spell
> woven of dead men's bones attracts to the scene of
> the massacre the present representations of a system
> doomed to vanish like that of the redskins before the
> advancing civilization of the new social era.[v]

ABOVE Known as the Massacre Tree, a cottonwood tree stood at the site of the Fort Dearborn Massacre. PAGE LEFT George Pullman invented the Pullman sleeping car, which became widely popular after it was attached to the funeral train that carried the body of President Abraham Lincoln to Illinois.

---  ⃝ᴥ⃝  ---

Superior's Flying Dutchman

The Curse of Copper

The C.G.S. Lambton—A Dangerous Design

The "Lighthouse of Doom"

# LAKE
# SUPERIOR

ABOVE The fate of the *Bannockburn* remains one of Lake Superior's great mysteries. The canaller was named in honor of the Scots who defeated a larger English force at Bannockburn in 1314. PAGE RIGHT Captain James McNaught of the steamer *Algonquin* spotted the *Bannockburn* about 50 miles (80kms) southwest of Passage Island, north-east of Keweenaw Point.

# Superior's Flying Dutchman

Captain McNaught of the steamer *Algonquin* may have been the last person to set eyes on the steamer *Bannockburn* on the afternoon of November 21, 1902. The *Bannockburn* was downbound from Port Arthur (now Thunder Bay), Ontario, and fighting a strong headwind when McNaught spotted it. The steamer belonged to a class of vessels given the name "canallers"; they were small enough (less than 250 feet in length) to fit through the Welland Canal. According to McNaught, the *Bannockburn* was running well... but when he looked up again a few moments later he could no longer see its three raking masts and tall funnel. The vessel was already out of sight! Later that night, the steady wind buffeting the bow of the canaller became a full-blown storm, one of the worst of the autumn season.

When the storm blew out, the *Bannockburn* was posted as overdue at the Sault Ste. Marie locks. Few were worried, however, as most assumed that Captain George R. Wood, an experienced master, had taken shelter along Superior's north shore and that the vessel would soon arrive in one piece. They also knew that the *Bannockburn* was a seaworthy vessel, built in 1893 in Middlesborough, Scotland, and rated AI by the insurers, Lloyds of London. The steamer had sailed Lake Superior for nine years, surviving every storm that the lake had churned out. But by November 27$^{th}$, six days after the vessel had set out, it was obvious that the *Bannockburn* was missing. The alarm was sounded all around the shores. Everyone had a theory as to the canaller's fate, and differing accounts in newspapers and telegrams caused mass confusion and speculation.

The *Fort Williams Times-Journal* published a story that had the *Bannockburn* lying behind Slate Island, but closer investigation proved there was no evidence of this—the story seemed pulled from thin air! On November 28$^{th}$ there was report of a steamer beached north of Michipicoten Island, but a thorough search brought up nothing. Meanwhile, in Kingston, Ontario, the owners of the missing vessel, the Montreal Transportation Company, received a wire from the Underwriter's Association in Chicago that read, "The steamer '*Bannockburn*' has been located on the north shore of Lake Superior, opposite Michipicoten Island. Crew safe." A company manager cheerfully relayed the good news to the families and friends of the crewmembers, and the Kingston newspaper reported, falsely, that everyone was alive and well. The Department of Customs in Ottawa received another telegram stating that the *Bannockburn* was ashore on Michipicoten Island.

After loading grain at Port Aurthor, the *Bannockburn* grounded.

Still other reports suggested that the *Bannockburn* might have foundered off Stannard Rock near the middle of Lake Superior, as the steamer *John D. Rockefeller* had passed through a wreckage field there on November 25th. Unfortunately, since the crew of the *Rockefeller* had not yet learned of the disappearance of the *Bannockburn*, they did not take particular note of the wreckage. This flotsam could not be conclusively linked to the missing steamer, but neither could it be discounted entirely.

There was talk too about the day that the *Bannockburn* had attempted to leave Port Arthur. Loaded down with 85,000 bushels of wheat from the Canadian Northern elevator, the steamer had grounded in the harbor. It did not appear to have sustained any major damage, and it finally cleared Port Arthur the following day. But perhaps there was a mistake. With the holds filled with wheat, it would have been impossible to have thoroughly inspected the hull. Could damages sustained in the incident have caused the ship to founder that night?

Captain McNaught of the *Algonquin* had another theory: the *Bannockburn*'s boilers had exploded, and the vessel had gone down quickly. How else to account for the disappearance of the ship before his own eyes on that afternoon? This could also help explain why none of the twenty crewmembers aboard survived; with so little warning, there would not have been time to grab life jackets or launch lifeboats. But then there was also the contradictory report from the pilothouse crew of the steamer *Huronic*, who sighted what they believed to be the *Bannockburn* on the night of the 21st, after McNaught had spotted it. Besides, many argued, the *Bannockburn* was only nine years old, too young for a boiler explosion.

On December 12th, Surfman Dean of the Grand Marais, Michigan, Life Saving Station found the only wreckage that could be positively identified: a single life jacket bearing the name *Bannockburn*. The strings were tied, suggesting that it had slipped from a body, but it could offer no clue as to how the canaller had been lost.

The loss of the *Bannockburn* remains one of the great mysteries of Lake Superior. In the century since its disappearance, no one has succeeded in locating the wreck. But people do claim to have seen

LEFT The *Bannockburn* is nicknamed for the *Flying Dutchman,* one of the most famous phantom ships. PAGE LEFT The crew of the steamer *Huronic* claimed to have passed the lights of the *Bannockburn* on the night of November 21st. If they were right, then Captain McNaught's theory that the *Bannockburn* went down earlier that day as a result of a boiler explosion cannot be valid.

the vessel live on in another guise… as a ghost ship. It is nicknamed the *Flying Dutchman,* after the schooner that was wrecked off the Cape of Good Hope and is said to reappear as a phantom ship. As soon as one year after the *Bannockburn's* disappearance, sailors began to report having seen its ghostly form steaming past Caribou Island, perhaps still trying to make it down to the Soo. Some early accounts tell of a "ghostly apparition of ice" seen "scudding through the gloom" on Lake Superior on stormy nights, "while in the darkened pilothouse her master looked vainly for the welcoming flash of Caribou Island Light."[i]

One more incident adds intrigue to the story of the lost *Bannockburn.* About 18 months after the disappearance there were reports that a trapper had come across a clue: an oar bearing the name *Bannockburn.* He found it buried behind a pile of driftwood, partially covered in a tarpaulin. Crude letters were carved deep into the wood of the oar shaft and, so legend contends, each letter was stained with human blood.

ABOVE   Five thousand years ago, prehistoric peoples on Lake Superior used giant stone hammers or "mauls" to separate copper ore from rock. Evidence of their mining is found throughout the Keweenaw Peninsula and on Isle Royale. PAGE RIGHT   Pictograph at Agawa Rock on the Canadian shore of Lake Superior depicting the underwater manitou Mishipeshu, guardian of Lake Superior's copper.

# The Curse of Copper

———— &c. ————

Many strong forces are at work on Lake Superior, natural and supernatural. The open water threatens to swallow vessels as though they were toys, and its rocky and forbidding shoreline stretches for many hundreds of miles. The earliest European missionaries and explorers to Superior heard tantalizing rumors of natural riches—deposits of native copper, an ore that is almost pure. Ojibwa spoke of islands where some masses of copper weighed up to 50 pounds (22.5kg) and were more than a foot long. The most fabled deposits were on Michipicoten Island and Isle Royale. But there were risks in stripping these islands of their treasure. The Ojibwa believed that Michipicoten Island was home to a powerful underworld manitou named Mishipeshu. This giant horned serpent (sometimes appearing as a horned lynx) watched over Superior's copper cache and

The "Ontonagon Boulder," a 3,708-lb. mass of pure copper, took 21 people one week to remove from the Ontonagon River. Today it is on display at the Smithsonian Institute.

meted out punishment to those who stole from him. He could travel around the Great Lakes through a series of underwater tunnels, and could whip still water into a fury.

In the *Jesuit Relations* of 1669–1670 Father Claude Dablon relates a story that was often repeated in the ensuing centuries. Four Ojibwa men camping on Michipicoten Island selected fine pieces of native copper, which, when heated and tossed into birchbark containers, were effective in bringing water to a boil. The men spent the night on the island without incident, but when they were canoeing away the next day with their copper riches, they were terrified to hear a thunderous voice boom out over the water saying, "Who are these robbers carrying off from me my children's cradles and play things?" Before they could reach the mainland, one of the men succumbed to a painful death. Two others died before the party could reach the village overland. The last man managed to survive long enough to report the incident to his village, but soon after arriving, he too surrendered to an agonizing death. This was put down to the work of Mishipeshu.

It is not surprising, then, that the Ojibwa feared the consequences of giving away the locations of the copper deposits. When, in

ABOVE A flatcar from a Keweenaw Peninsula mine takes mass copper to the smelter. LOWER Douglass Houghton came to Michigan in 1830 to give a series of scientific lectures. In 1842 he was elected Mayor of Detroit.

1798, explorer David Thompson asked to be shown the place of one legendary copper deposit, his Ojibwa guides "said they did not exactly know it, and dreaded the Musquitoes...." So the copper in the Lake Superior region was safe from extraction on a large scale... that is, until the 1840s, when a 3,708-pound copper boulder was found at Ontonagon, on the American south shore. The Keweenaw Peninsula became the focus of North America's first great mining boom.

Michigan state geologist Douglass Houghton was arguably the man most responsible for causing the thousands of prospectors and miners to flood into the region. Beginning in 1838 he surveyed

The deep pitting on this 6,000-lb. copper mass is from the hammer strikes of prehistoric miners.

the Lower and Upper Keweenaw Peninsula, and it was his 1841 report that sparked things off. Not surprisingly, it was Houghton himself who met head on with the copper curse in October of 1845. He was finishing his survey, when on the morning of the 13th he left Eagle Harbor, Michigan, in a rowboat with Oliver Larrimer and Tousin Piquette, heading for a point about 15 miles (24km) to the west. Grey skies and intermittent snow were not threatening enough to keep Houghton from completing his work. The trip out was made without incident, and at sundown Houghton began the return trip to Eagle Harbor with Larrimer, Piquette and two voyageurs, Peter McFarlane and John B. Bodrie. Larrimer was scheduled to board the *Napolean* at Eagle or Agate Harbor, and he was anxious to return in time to meet the vessel.

With Houghton steering and the four men rowing, the party made decent progress, but before long, the wind came up and the snow grew heavier. Passing a sandbank, McFarlane suggested they go ashore for the night. Houghton persuaded them to continue, as they were not far from the settlement of Eagle River, where Larrimer could meet his ship and where the rest of them could stop for the night at a log house. The wind stiffened from the northeast, and, fighting the

Houghton, Michigan, was a copper-mining town and the major shipping center for the region. It was named after Douglass Houghton.

breakers, the little boat began to take on water. McFarlane advised Houghton to put on his life jacket. Struggling with the tiller, Houghton placed the jacket aside until he could get a free hand. Waves were swamping the boat, and Houghton had no choice but to turn in and risk a landing on a now rocky shore.

They didn't make it. Out from the rocks, two large waves capsized the vessel. McFarlane surfaced first and grabbed hold of the keel. Seeing an arm under the boat, he reached down and dragged Houghton to the keel by his collar. "Never mind me, try to get to shore if you can. I will get ashore well enough" were Houghton's last words to McFarlane as a massive wave struck the boat. McFarlane managed to gain the boat again and saw that Bodrie was hanging on to the bow. Another wave struck, and both men were torn from the overturned craft. They managed to make it to shore but could not locate the others.

The next morning some sixty searchers combed the coastline for the missing men. They found the body of Tousin Piquette and pieces of the boat. Houghton's body washed ashore the following spring, and he was later buried in Detroit's Elmwood cemetery.

Through the next eighty years, the Keweenaw Peninsula was one of the most important copper-producing areas in the world. Vessels plied the waters along Superior's south shore, carrying Lake Superior copper to markets back east. The copper curse followed them. Many copper-laden vessels were lost, including the *Pewabic* and the *Kitty Reeves*.

Over a period of fifty years, about ten divers lost their lives trying to recover the cache. ∞

On August 9, 1865, the 200-foot (60-m) steamer *Pewabic* was traveling on Lake Huron to Cleveland with a full load of copper and passengers when it met with disaster off Alpena, Michigan. Through an error in navigation, the *Pewabic* and its sister ship, the *Meteor*, collided in broad daylight. The *Meteor* holed the *Pewabic*, which sank within minutes. Some passengers on board the *Pewabic* managed to climb over to the *Meteor*, and others were rescued from the water. Captain McKay of the *Pewabic* crossed over just before his ship dove to the bottom of the lake. Reports state that no sooner had he arrived on the *Meteor's* deck than he accused Captain Wilson, who was directing the rescue efforts, of wanting to drown them all "in order that there might be no one to testify at an investigation." A cause for the disaster was never proven. Whoever was to blame, the *Pewabic* took down with it about 100 passengers and the ship's cargo of 200 tons of pure copper.

Even from the lake bottom, the *Pewabic* continued to claim more lives. Salvagers were lured to the site by the valuable copper, as well as by a purser's safe said to hold $50,000 in gold. Over a period of fifty years, about ten divers lost their lives trying to recover the cache.

An 1897 shipping notice announced that the wreck of the *Pewabic* had been found in 27 fathoms of water. That year, the Aetna Insurance Company (stung by the $61,000 *Pewabic* claim) hired a salvage company to retrieve its copper. A team examined the wreck from a newly designed diving bell that had a glass bottom and sides. Equipped with "telephonic communications," the bell also had grappling hooks on the end of two steel rods to handle wreckage. The insurance agent who was along for the ride saw no copper in the ship's hold. He surmised that when the *Pewabic* sank, shifting ore smashed through the hull and became trapped beneath it. They managed to retrieve thirty tons of the ore, the most substantial boulder weighing a hefty 11,200 pounds.

One ambitious salvager, Dr. Fernando Staud of Chicago, had a plan to float the vessel to the surface by sinking huge tanks with chains around the wreck, and pumping air into the tanks. But after three months of battling with poor weather, the expedition was called off without a single pound of copper recovered. In 1917, the Leavitt Deep Sea Diving Company picked up where Staud left off. After weeks of dragging the lake bottom, they finally relocated the *Pewabic,* and sent down Oliver H. Shirley, chief diver on the expedition, to survey the wreck. Swimming through corridors and staterooms, he found skeletons, dishes still in their racks, passengers' trunks... but not the safe. A large hole in the floor of the purser's cabin led Shirley to believe that when the *Pewabic* slammed into the lake bottom, the heavy safe had crashed through to the fo'c'sle. He returned to the surface excited by his discoveries.

During the next week, the team anchored a barge at the site and set out permanent buoys. Crews made several dives, and in the evening they even dined on canned delicacies and drank beer that had been at the bottom of the lake for fifty years! Over time the salvage crew brought up about 150 tons of copper before a problem arose. A rumor circulated that the U.S. Government had claimed title to the copper. The U.S. had just entered World War I, and copper was an important material in the war effort. The Leavitt Company gave up its operation and left the salvaged copper on the dock in Alpena, Michigan. (Some historians contend that a more likely explanation is that since the price of copper was frozen during the war, it had become of little value to the salvagers.)

The schooner *Kitty Reeves* also lies on the bottom of Lake Huron with its cargo of copper ingots. Had Mishipeshu followed the schooner here? On November 7, 1870, the *Reeves* sank during a heavy gale off Tawas Point at the northern end of Saginaw Bay. The waves and wind were battering the *Reeves*, and they were losing steerage. The crew dropped anchor in an attempt to keep the vessel's nose in the wind, and they managed to launch and beach the lifeboat—both miraculous feats. But then they watched as the storm snapped their vessel's anchor chain, and waves wreacked havoc on the hull, sinking it in a few hours along with the entire cargo of copper ingots. For many years afterwards, the schooner's mast was visible underwater on calm days, until ice eventually shifted this clue and the location of the vessel was lost. But the memory of the vessel, and of its precious cargo, was not.

Over eighty years later, in August 1952, two expeditions claimed to have discovered the wreck. One was led by Saginaw oil-lease broker Wilford G. Shannon, and the other by an 82-year-old retired general store keeper from Danbury, Ohio, named Julius Roth. The crews were anchored only a quarter mile (0.4km) from one another, and each was adamant that it was floating above the *Reeves*. Roth had spent ten years researching the wreck and had tracked down a man named Frank Black who, as a young boy, had witnessed the *Reeves* at anchor off Tawas Point on the stormy November night it went down. Using Black's information and weather data from the U.S. Weather Bureau, Roth approximated the location of the wreck. He then used a pair of underwater metal detectors to find what he believed to be the schooner. Gossip on shore and even across the country was that Shannon was cheating by moving his crew in after Roth had done the research.

The battle between the two expeditions became fierce, and each issued statements to the press in an attempt to prove that its site held the wreck of the *Reeves*. Roth acquired a sandsucker in Toledo to try and uncover his wreck, but the derelict vessel sank soon after arriving. Meanwhile, Shannon announced that his divers had drilled into wood, presumably the *Reeves*. Both men knew that they would need sandsuckers and clamshell power shovels if they had any chance of uncovering their wrecks. However, bad weather put a stop to exploration for that year, and the crews packed up for the winter. Soon after, Roth took ill and had to quit his work. Neither team returned to Tawas Point, and the copper remained undisturbed.

Perhaps the Ojibwa were right to dread the consequences of stealing copper from Mishipeshu, Superior's vengeful underwater manitou.

The *Lambton* was built in 1909 in Sorel, Quebec. It measured 108 feet (32.4m) long, 25 feet (7.5m) wide and had a 90 horsepower Triple Expansion Steam Engine.

# The C.G.S. Lambton
# A Dangerous Design

⟡

The story of the C.G.S. *Lambton* revolves around perhaps the most secluded lighthouse on the Great Lakes, Caribou Island lighthouse. Caribou is 65 miles (104 km) out on treacherous Lake Superior from the nearest port, Michipicoten Harbor. George Johnston kept the light from 1912 to 1921, and stories of his ingenuity abound (a necessary trait at so isolated a posting). When he broke his leg, he set the bone himself and applied a splint to the wound. Devising a makeshift peg leg and crutches, he still managed to climb the steep lighthouse ladder to attend to the lantern.

His resourcefulness was never more tested, however, than at the end of the shipping season in 1915. That year, Lake Superior keepers were informed that the government would no longer provide a vessel to drop them off and pick them up at the beginning and end of the navigation season. Instead, each lightkeeper was to be issued a 28-foot (8.4m) sailboat to make the trip to and from the lights on their own. For Johnston, this meant traveling over 65 miles (104kms) on Lake Superior in December in a small open sailboat! Johnston got

ABOVE Rebuilt in 1911, the Caribou lighttower measured 90 feet (27m) high. Lightkeeper George Johnston managed to climb the tower even with a broken leg. LOWER George Johnston.

right to work improving his odds of survival. He bought a kerosene engine for the boat, built a small cabin from scrap lumber and canvas, and even added a coal heater. Despite these preparations, four years later, while attempting to return to the mainland at the end of season, Johnston and his assistant were trapped in ice for seven harrowing days. Miraculously, they finally reached shore on New Year's Day.

Johnston took the job of fog alarm inspector a few years later, and in 1921 he trained a new lightkeeper, George Penefold, for the post at Caribou Island. Penefold was shocked to learn that the government expected him to make his own way off the light in December in the small boat. He directed an angry letter-writing campaign to the authorities and succeeded in convincing them to reverse their policy. The government

George Johnston, and then his wife Louise, wrote to the government to warn that the *Lambton* was not safe as a lighthouse tender.

acquiesced by commissioning the 108-foot (32.4m) *Lambton* as a lighthouse tender, responsible for lighthouse supply from Quebec north to the Upper Great Lakes. Penefold had won the battle... so it seemed.

That autumn, Johnston witnessed a shocking scene that prompted him to write to the same authorities. The *Lambton* was the wrong choice for a lighthouse tender. He saw the vessel's crew chipping ice off the steering cable. Originally designed as a tug, the boat sat low in the water, and the steering quadrant was susceptible to freezing spray. In addition, the ship's lifeboats were positioned on the uppermost deck, far out of reach during a storm. When Johnston's letter was ignored, his wife Louise took up the campaign. She explained that the family could not afford life insurance on Johnston's wages. Theirs was a large family, and should anything happen to her

PAGE RIGHT The *Lambton*. ABOVE Originally built as a tug, the *Lambton* rode low in the water. This was dangerous on the open water, as the steering quadrant was exposed to freezing spray.

husband, they would be in dire straits. Her efforts, too, were ignored, and the *Lambton* remained scheduled to drop off Lake Superior keepers in the spring. Johnston, however, did not climb aboard.

The *Lambton* left Sault Ste. Marie on Tuesday April 18, 1922, with keepers for the lighthouses at Ile Parisienne, Caribou Island (including George Penefold) and Michipicoten Island. In all, 22 people were on board, along with supplies for the season. Whitefish Bay was still an icefield, and the steamer *Glenfinnan* ran into trouble trying to weave its way through. The *Lambton* was nearby, and in the process of going to the steamer's assistance, the *Lambton* collided with it. The captain of the *Glenfinnan* later reported that the tender did not sustain

any damage from the collision but that the *Lambton's* steering gear was damaged at some point before the two vessels cleared the ice. Instead of returning to port to make repairs, the crew rigged makeshift steering lines and continued on its way. On the afternoon of April 19th, the *Lambton*, the *Glenfinnan* and its sister ship, the *Glenlivet*, were within sight of one another about 35 miles (56km) past Whitefish Point. Then a spring storm advanced, and the weather began rapidly deteriorating. The two steamers turned back to take shelter behind the point. Only minutes after they reached safety, a full-blown gale struck. The *Lambton*, however, forged on.

Large steamers saw the tender about forty miles (64km) from Whitefish Point struggling with the broken steering gear. In such a situation, one can only speculate as to why the captain of the *Lambton* decided to brave the storm. With navigation starting up for the season, did he feel responsible for getting the lightkeepers to their posts as soon as possible? The last vessel to see the *Lambton* was the steamer *Midland Prince*. Officers saw the tender fighting the gale as the wind shifted from south-

On April 18, 1922, the *Lambton* collided with the steamer *Glenfinnan* in Whitefish Bay while trying to free the steamer from the ice. At some point between the collision and clearing the bay the *Lambton*'s steering gear was damaged.

east to northeast and built to one of the worst they had ever experienced. When the wind died down, they had lost sight of the tender.

There was no word of the *Lambton* for five days. On April 23rd, the downbound steamer *Valcartier* reported that early on the morning of the 20th they had passed what looked like the top of a pilothouse painted white and trimmed with red about 25 miles (40km) southeast of Michipicoten Island and 15 miles (24km) east of Caribou Island. *Valcartier's* wheelsman had sailed on the *Lambton* before and was certain that the pilothouse belonged to the missing tender.

The Canadian Superintendent of Lights, J. N. Arthurs, hired the tug *G. R. Gray* to conduct a search, but the tug could not move from Point aux Pins until an upbound freighter broke a path through the spring ice on April 25th. Each hour they lost was crucial. Was there a chance that anyone could have survived for six days by floating on the wreckage? Could any of them have managed to reach shore and shelter themselves? The chances were slim, but the search team continued their efforts for five days before giving up hope. Johnston was among the searchers, and we can only imagine his disgust at the tragedy. His party discovered one of the *Lambton's* lifeboats. Its air tanks had been crushed, suggesting that it had still been attached to the top deck when the tender dove into the lake. The pressure of the descent would have collapsed the tanks before the boat broke loose. Johnston's concerns about the *Lambton* proved eerily accurate: the lifeboats were out of reach of the crew as the boat went down, and it appeared that the broken steering gear contributed to the vessel's demise.

Although the *Lambton* and all aboard were never seen again, many believe that the lighthouse tender lives on as a ghost ship that still sails Lake Superior. In August 1922, Captain John McPherson saw the ghostly form of the *Lambton* off Cape Gargantua while sailing on the tug *Reliance*. Others confirmed his sighting from shore. Mrs. Charles Miron, the wife of the lightkeeper at Gargantua, saw the ghostly vessel through binoculars and was certain it was the *Lambton*.

Mr. and Mrs. Charles Graham also spotted the phantom ship. Between sunset and sunrise, the tender is said to appear as a phantom white shape—perhaps its captain is still trying to deliver the lightkeepers to their posts, so they can help other vessels in need.

The crew of the steamer *Valcartier* believed they saw the pilothouse of the *Lambton* floating in the water on the 20th of April.

The lighthouse on Talbot Island was one of six built on Lakes Huron and Superior in 1867, around the time of Confederation. Its boxy design was like the one shown here from Killarney, Georgian Bay. None of these six original wooden lighthouses survive.

# St. Ignace Light
## The "Lighthouse of Doom"

⟨⟩

Named for nearby St. Ignace Island, the "lighthouse of doom," as it has been dubbed, was the first Canadian lighthouse on Lake Superior. It was one of six new lighthouses planned "on the line of navigation followed by vessels running from Collingwood to the head of Lake Superior," to be erected and completed in the summer of 1867. Most were on Lake Huron; the St. Ignace lighthouse was to be the only one along the entire Canadian coast of Superior. Canada was a new country in 1867, and building these lights in such remote locations was an impressive feat—but things did not go well at the St. Ignace light. Ironically, a scant six years after it was built, the light was decommissioned because it had been the *cause* of too much loss of life. What went wrong?

The lighthouse was a square white wooden tower built on a rocky clearing on long, narrow Talbot Island. Three kerosene lamps threw a light to warn sailors of shoals in the area. The lighthouse was extremely remote—over 200 miles (320km) from Sault Ste. Marie. Since returning the lightkeeper back to the Sault would have to be done before the winter freeze-up, this would mean closing down the lighthouse before the end of the navigation season. As this would put some

Talbot Island is so overgrown that the lighthouse foundation is no longer visible.

ships in peril, officials decided that the light-keeper would have to wait until after the navigation season closed, and then make his own way off the island to winter quarters. A logical decision, but also a deadly one.

Disaster struck quickly. A Mr. Perry tended the light during the inaugural 1867 season, and the 1868 annual report of the Department of Marine and Fisheries tells his story:

> During the year a change took place among keepers, namely the death of Mr. Perry of St. Ignace light in Lake Superior. At the close of navigation in November 1867, Mr. Perry extinguished his light and started in an open boat for one of the posts of the Hudson's Bay Company at Nipigon. He perished on the way. His body was found in the spring near his boat, on the mainland in Nipigon, about fourteen miles, from the posts for which he was making his way.

The St. Ignace light had claimed its first victim.

The next keeper, Mr. Thomas Lampier, tried an alternate plan. He and his wife had a residence built on the island, where they planned to stay year-round. The winter would be very long, with no letters, visitors or supply boats, but the Lampiers felt up to the chal-

ABOVE Silver Islet mine was located just off the mainland town of the same name (seen right). Fishermen on the Silver Islet dock noticed light-keeper Andrew Hynes' empty sailboat.

lenge. Their forti-
tude, however, was
not enough to
counter the ill luck that shrouded the light. During their first winter, Mr. Lampier fell sick and died. Unable to bury the body of her
husband in the frozen ground, Mrs. Lampier wrapped him in canvas and placed him in a rock crevice behind the buildings. The poor
woman lived alone with the body all winter until she was discovered
in the spring. A native woman from Hudson Bay, her long black
hair had turned white during the ordeal—"the winter took it," was
all she offered as explanation. As Talbot Island was so rocky, her
husband was buried on nearby Bowman Island, about a mile
(1.6km) to the north.

The next two years passed without incident, but the fall of 1872 brought further tragedy. The Department of Marine and Fisheries reported that the lightkeeper, Mr. Andrew Hynes, had struggled to reach the mining community of Silver Islet at the end of the navigation season. When fishermen on the Silver Islet dock noticed his sailboat moving slowly towards them, they hailed it—but there was no response. Reaching the boat, they found Hynes draped over the tiller, barely conscious. It had taken him 18 days to travel over fifty miles (80km), and soon after arriving, he died from "the effects of exposure which he had undergone." The Department had had enough, concluding:

> He was the second keeper who perished in endeavoring to return from this station; and owing to this fact, and to the light now being of comparatively little importance to navigation on Lake Superior, it has been decided to discontinue it; and to erect other lights of more importance to the present growing trade.

The first three keepers had died in the short period of six years, and the Department was not going to allow this cursed lighthouse to take any further victims.

Fishermen established camps in the area in the 1880s, and although the light was dormant, they still used the lighthouse as a visual reference point. On days when fog blanketed the area, men would row to the old tower and bang on its wooden sides to guide the fishing boats home. The abandoned lighthouse also became the site of a strange specter. Fishermen have described moonlit nights where they have seen a woman with pure white hair walking along Talbot's shore and calling out softly. Had the spirit of Mrs. Lampier stayed on the island to warn others of the dangers lurking there?

Today, little remains on Talbot Island to mark the site of the "lighthouse of doom." Lake Superior's harsh climate has long since toppled the wooden structure, and the moss-covered forest has crept in, covering the small clearing where so much tragedy was exacted over one hundred years ago. The only artifact that remains is on Bowman Island—Thomas Lampier's grave, marked by a simple white cross.

ABOVE    Bill    Schelling inspects foundation of lighthouse on Talbot Island, c. 1960s.    LEFT    Keeper Thomas Lampier was buried on nearby Bowman Island.

# Endnotes

## Introduction

[i]*Hugh Cochrane, Gateway to Oblivion: The Great Lakes' Bermuda Triangle. (Toronto: Doubleday Canada Limited), 1980.*

## Fox Sisters and Modern Spiritualism

[i] Barbara M. Weiber, "They Spoke With the Dead." *American Heritage.* Vol. 50, No. 5, September 1999, pp. 84-92.

[ii] Ibid.

[iii]Ibid.

[iv]John Robert Colombo, *Mysterious Canada.* (Toronto: Doubleday Canada Limited), 1988.

[v] David Chapin, "The Fox Sisters and the Mystery of Performance." *American History.* Vol. 81, No. 2, 2000, pp. 156-188.

[vi]Colombo, *Mysterious Canada.*

[vii] Ibid.

[viii] Weiber, "They Spoke With the Dead."

## Lily of the Prince George Hotel

[i] Terry Boyle, *Haunted Ontario.* (Toronto: Polar Bear Press), 1988.

[ii] Ibid.

## Speedy

[i] Hugh Cochrane, *Gateway to Oblivion: The Great Lakes' Bermuda Triangle.* (Toronto: Doubleday Canada Limited), 1980.

[ii] Brendan O'Brien, *Speedy Justice: The Tragic Last Voyage of His Magesty's Vessel Speedy.* (Toronto: University of Toronto Press), 1992.

[iii] C.H.J. Snider, "Schooner Days," *Toronto Telegram.* Jan 15, 1949.

## Gibraltar Point Lighthouse

[i] Frederick Stonehouse, *Haunted Lakes: Great Lakes Ghost Stories, Superstitions and Sea Serpents.* (Chelsea, Michigan: Lake Superior Port Cities Inc.), 1997.

[ii] *Toronto Telegram,* April 19, 1926

## Hamilton & Scourge

[i] Frederick Stonehouse, *Haunted Lakes: Great Lakes Ghost Stories, Superstitions and Sea Serpents.* (Chelsea, Michigan: Lake Superior Port Cities Inc.), 1997.

## The Black Dog of Lake Erie

[i] C.H.J. Snider, "Schooner Days," *Toronto Telegram,* September 26, 1931.

[ii] C.H.J. Snider, "Schooner Days," *Toronto Telegram,* 1930.

[iii] Ibid.

[iv] Ibid.

## Johnson's Island

[i] Kathleen Warnes, "Confederate Prisoners of War on Lake Erie," *Inland Seas.* Winter 1996, pp. 302-310.

[ii]Roger Long, "Johnson's Island Prison," *Blue & Gray Magazine.* Vol. 4, No. 4, Feb-March 1987.

[iv] Andrea Gutsche & Cindy Bisaillon, *Mysterious Islands: Forgotten Tales of the Great Lakes.* (Toronto: Lynx Images Inc.), 1999.

## Kelleys Island Quarry

[i] Frederick Stonehouse, *Haunted Lakes II: More Great Lakes Ghost Stories.* (Chelsea, Michigan: Lake Superior Port Cities Inc.), 2000.

[ii] Ibid.

[iii] Ibid.

## Convict Ship Success

[i] Frederick Stonehouse, *Haunted Lakes: Great Lakes Ghost Stories, Superstitions and Sea Serpents.* (Chelsea, Michigan: Lake Superior Port Cities Inc.), 1997.

[ii] Ibid.

## One Bride's Nightmare—Waubuno

[i] C.H.J. Snider, "Schooner Days," *Toronto Telegram,* Jan 10, 1953. Other sources indicate that the word *waubuno* means black magic.

## Waubuno Continued

ii Frederick Stonehouse, *Haunted Lakes II: More Great Lakes Ghost Stories*. (Chelsea, Michigan: Lake Superior Port Cities Inc.), 2000.

## Le Griffon

i Dwight Boyer, *Great Stories of the Great Lakes*. (New York: Dodd, Mead & Company), 1966.

ii Ibid.

iii Andrea Gutsche, Barbara Chisholm & Russell Floren, *Alone in the Night: Lighthouses of Georgian Bay, Manitoulin Island and the North Channel*. (Toronto: Lynx Images Inc.), 1996, pp.254-257.

iv Frederick Stonehouse, *Haunted Lakes: Great Lakes Ghost Stories, Superstitions and Sea Serpents*. (Chelsea, Michigan: Lake Superior Port Cities Inc.), 2000.

## A Sailor's Hunch—Our Son

i C.H.J. Snider, "Schooner Days," *Toronto Telegram*, February 10, 1934.

ii Dwight Boyer, *Ghost Ships of the Great Lakes*. (New York: Dodd, Mead & Company), 1968.

iii Ibid.

iv Ibid.

## She has Gone to Pieces—Chicora

i Dwight Boyer, *Ghost Ships of the Great Lakes*. (New York: Dodd, Mead & Company), 1968.

ii Ibid.

ii Ibid.

iv Frederick, *Went Missing*. (Marquette, MI: Avery Color Studios), 1984.

## Fort Dearborn Massacre

i Ursula Bielski, *Chicago Haunts: Ghostlore of the Windy City*. (Chicago: Lake Claremont Press), 1998.

ii Ibid.

iii Ibid.

## Fort Dearborn Massacre Continued

iv Ibid.

v Donald L. Miller, *City of the Century: The Epic of Chicago and the Making of America*. (Toronto: Simon & Schuster), 1996.

## Flying Dutchman—Bannockburn

i George W. Stark, "A Century of Steam on the Great Lakes," *Outlook*, July, 1917.

## The Curse of Copper

i Barbara Chisholm & Andrea Gutsche, *Superior: Under the Shadow of the Gods*. (Toronto: Lynx Images Inc.), 1999.

ii Ibid.

iii By all accounts, Houghton was an outstanding citizen. He came to Michigan in 1830 to give a series of scientific lectures and eventually settled in Detroit. Houghton became a popular leader in the community: he helped found the Detroit Young Man's Society in 1833, he was an active member of the Episcopal Church, the first president of the Detroit Board of Education and was appointed professor of the young University of Michigan. In 1842 he was elected Mayor of Detroit.

iv The *Meteor* was only slightly damaged in the collision and, after minor repairs, the vessel continued on. However, two days later while tied up at Sault Ste. Marie, water seeped into the hull and reacted with the cargo of lime causing a fire. The passengers and crew managed to escape but the vessel had to be scuttled in the St. Mary's River.

# Selective Bibliography

Atkins, Kenneth S. *"Le Griffon:* A New View" *Inland Seas.* (Vermilion, Ohio: Great Lakes Historical Society) Vol. 46, No. 3, 1990, pp.162-169.

Avery, Thomas. *Copper Country—God's Country: Reflections on a Unique Land and its Metal.* (Michigan: Avery Color Studios), 1973.

Bielski, Ursula. *Chicago Haunts: Ghostlore of the Windy City.* (Chicago: Lake Claremont Press), 1998.

Boyer, Dwight. *Ghost Ships of the Great Lakes.* (New York: Dodd, Mead & Company), 1968.

_____. *Strange Adventures of the Great Lakes.* (New York: Dodd, Mead & Company), 1968.

_____. *Great Stories of the Great Lakes.* (New York: Dodd, Mead & Company), 1966.

Boyle, Terry. *Haunted Ontario.* (Toronto: Polar Bear Press), 1998.

Burton, Clarence M. "The Fort Dearborn Massacre" *Magazine of History with Notes and Queries.* (New York: W. Abbatt), Vol. 15, No. 2 & No. 3, pp.74-76, 85-96.

Chapin, David. "The Fox Sisters and the Mystery of Performance." *American History.* (Harrisburg, Pennsylvania: Cowles History Group, a division of Cowles Magazines), Vol. 81, No. 2, 2000, pp.156-188.

Chaput, Donald. "Michipicton Island: Ghosts, Copper and Bad Luck." *Ontario History.* (Toronto: Ontario Historical Society), Vol. 61, No. 3, 1969, pp.217-223.

Chisholm, Barbara & Andrea Gutsche. *Superior: Under the Shadow of the Gods.* (Toronto: Lynx Images Inc.), 1999.

Clark, Ella Elizabeth. *Indian Legends of Canada.* (Toronto: McClelland and Stewart Limited), 1960.

Cochrane, Hugh. *Gateway to Oblivion: The Great Great Lakes' Bermuda Triangle.* (Toronto: Doubleday Canada Limited), 1980.

Colombo, John Robert. *Ghost Stories of Canada.* (Toronto: A Hounslow Book, The Dundurn Group), 2000.

_____. *Ghost Stories of Ontario.* (Toronto: Hounslow Press), 1995.

_____. *Mysterious Canada.* (Toronto: Doubleday Canada Limited), 1988.

Dean, Pauline. *Sagas of Superior the Island Sea. . .and its Canadian Shore.* (Manitouwadge, Ontario: Great Spirit Writers), 1992.

Dickson, Kenneth. *"The Flying Dutchman* of Lake Superior." *Inland Seas.* (Vermilion, Ohio: Great Lakes Historical Society), Vol. 50, No. 2, 1994, pp.104-110.

Francis, David W. "Johnson's Island: A History of the Resort Era" *Inland Seas.* (Vermilion, Ohio: Great Lakes Historical Society), Vol. 36, No. 4, 1980, pp.257-263.

Gibson, Sally. *More Than an Island: A History of the Toronto Island.* (Toronto: Irwin Publishing), 1984.

Gutsche, Andrea & Cindy Bisaillon. *Mysterious Islands: Forgotten Tales of the Great Lakes.* (Toronto: Lynx Images Inc.), 1999.

Gutsche, Andrea, Barbara Chisholm & Russell Floren. *The North Channel and St. Mary's River: A Guide to the History.* (Toronto: Lynx Images Inc.), 1997.

Gutsche, Andrea, Barbara Chisholm & Russell Floren. *Alone in the Night: Lighthouses of Georgian Bay, Manitoulin Island and the North Channel.* (Toronto: Lynx Images Inc.), 1996.

Havighurst, Walter, Ed. *The Great Lakes Reader.* (New York: The Macmillan Company), 1966.

Hyde, Charles K. *The Northern Lights: Lighthouses of the Upper Great Lakes.* (Lansing, Michigan: Two Peninsula Press), 1986.

Krause, David J. "Testing a Tradition: Douglass Houghton and the Native Copper of Lake Superior" *ISIS.* (Chicago: The University of Chicago Press), 1989, Vol. 80. No. 304, pp.622-639.

Lambert, R.S. *Exploring the Supernatural: The Weird in Canadian Folklore.* (Toronto: McClelland & Stewart Ltd.), 1955.

Lindquist, Kirk and Saralee R. Howard-Filler. "Douglass Houghton: The Man and the Painting" *Michigan History.* (Lansing, Michigan: Michigan History Division of the Dept. of State), Vol. 71, No. 6, p. 12-19.

Litteljohn, Bruce and Wayland Drew. *The Haunted Shore.* (Toronto: Gage Publishing Limited), 1975.

Long, Roger. "Johnson's Island Prison" *Blue & Gray Magazine.* (Columbus, Ohio: Blue & Gray Enterprises), Vol. 4, No. 4, Feb-March 1987.

McKean, Fleetwood K. "The Wreck of the SS *Waubuno*" *Inland Seas.* (Vermilion, Ohio: Great Lakes Historical Society), Vol. 21, No. 4, 1965, pp.302-304.

Miller, Donald L. *City of the Century: The Epic of Chicago and the Making of America.* (Toronto: Simon & Schuster), 1996.

Murphy, Rowley W. "Ghosts of the Great Lakes: Part I" *Inland Seas.* (Vermilion, Ohio: Great Lakes Historical Society), Summer 1961, pp.88-96.

Nelson, Dan. "The Sinking of the *Hamilton* and *Scourge*—How Many Men Were Lost" *Freshwater.* (Navarre, Minnesota: Freshwater Biological Research Foundation), Vol. 2, No.1, p 4-7.

O'Brien, Brendan. *Speedy Justice: The Tragic Last Voyage of His Majesty's Vessel Speedy.* (TorontoUniversity of Toronto Press), 1992.

Osborne, A.C. "The Migration of Voyageurs from Drummond Island to Penetanguishene in 1828" *Ontario Historical Society Papers and Records, Vol III.* (Toronto: Ontario Historical Society), 1901.

Palmer, Richard F. "The *General Hamilton* and the *Scourge*" *Inland Seas.* (Vermilion, Ohio: Great Lakes Historical Society), Vol. 35, No. 3, 1979, pp.192-195.

Quife, Milo Milton. "Fort Dearborn and Its Story" *The Dial.* (New York: Dial Press), Vol. 53, July-Dec. 1912, pp.129-131.

Ratigan, William. *Great Lakes Shipwrecks & Survivals.* (Grand Rapids, Michigan: William B. Eerdmans Publishing Co.), 1977.

Reed, Christopher R. "In the Shadow of Fort Dearborn: Honoring Du Sable at the Chicago World's Fair of 1933-1934." *Journal of Black Studies.* (Newbury Park, California: Sage Publications, Inc.), Vol. 21, No. 4, June 1991, pp.398-413.

Sangster, Dorothy. "Raising the *Hamilton* and *Scourge*" *Canadian Geographic.* (Toronto: Canadian Geographic Enterprises), Vol. 103, No. 1, pp.22-29.

Shepard, Frederick J. "The Johnson's Island Plot" *Publications of the Buffalo Historical Society,* Vol. IX. (Buffalo: Buffalo Historical Society), 1906.

Sieber, Robert, Kathy Peterson & Marjorie Searl, Eds. "The Fox Sisters in Action: A Clergyman's Account" *New York History.* (Albany, New York: New York State Historical Association), Vol. 33, No. 3, pp.310-318.

# Selective Bibliography

Sigurdson, Jim. "Lighthouse of Doom." *Thunder Bay Historical Society Papers to 1967.* (Thunder Bay, Ontario: Thunder Bay Historical Society), 1967.

Stead, Frank E. "The First Season's Work: A Summary of Dr. Douglass Houghton's 1827 Geological Survey of Michigan's Lower Peninsula" *Michigan Historical Review.* (Mount Pleasant, Michigan: Clarke Historical Library at Central Michigan University in cooperation with the Historical Society of Michigan), Vol. 20, No. 1, pp.80-94.

Steer, Don. *Superior's East Shore: Mamainse to Gargantua.* (Sault Ste. Marie: Don Steer), 1995.

Stonehouse, Frederick. *Haunted Lakes: Great Lakes Ghost Stories, Superstitions and Sea Serpents.* (Chelsea, Michigan: Lake Superior Port Cities Inc.), 1997.

_____. *Haunted Lakes II: More Great Lakes Ghost Stories.* (Chelsea, Michigan: Lake Superior Port Cities Inc.), 2000.

_____. *Went Missing: Unsolved Great Lakes Shipwreck Mysteries.* (Marquette, MI: Avery Color Studios), 1984.

Turcott, Agnes W. *Land of the Big Goose: A History of Wawa and the Michipicoten Area.* (Dryden, Ontario: Alec Wilson Publications), 1962.

Wakefield, Larry. "Drummond Island" *Chronicle: The Quarterly Magazine of the Historical Society of Michigan.* Vol. 21, No. 4, 1985, pp.2-7.

Warner, Robert M. "The Drowning of Douglass Houghton" *Inland Seas.* (Vermilion, Ohio: Great Lakes Historical Society), 1970, Vol. 26, No. 2, pp.118-122.

Warnes, Kathleen. "Confederate Prisoners of War on Lake Erie" *Inland Seas.* (Vermilion, Ohio: Great Lakes Historical Society), Winter 1996, pp.302-310.

Weiber, Barbara M. "They Spoke With the Dead" *American Heritage.* (Cooperstown, New York: American Association for State and Local History), Vol. 50, No. 5, September 1999, pp.84-92.

Williams, W. R. "*The* Jane Miller *Mystery*" *Inland Seas.* (Vermilion, Ohio: Great Lakes Historical Society), Vol. 21, No. 4, 1965, pp.300-301.

Wilson, John S. "Emerson and the Rochester Rappings" *The New England Quarterly.* (Boston, MA: The New England Quarterly), Vol. 41, No. 2, pp.248-258.

Wright, Larry & Patricia. *Bonfires & Beacons: Great Lakes Lighthouses.* (Erin, Ontario: The Boston Mills Press), 1996.

# Index

# Index

# Picture Credits

Archives of Ontario: 74
Bruce County Museum and Archives: 82, 84
Burton Historical Collection, Detroit Public Library: 146
City of Toronto Archives: 36(m)
Collingwood Museum: 76,
Follett House: 54(t,b), 56, 57, 58, 59(m), 63(t)
Historical Collections of the Great Lakes, Bowling Green State University: 118
Hoyland, Dorothy : 160
Huronia Museum/Mississagi Strait Lighthouse Museum: 107, 109
Imperial Oil Collection: 24
Johnston, Pat/Lynx Images: 154(t,b), 155, 157
Kelleys Island Historical Society: 60, 62, 63(b), 65
Lynx Images Inc.: 38, 59(i), 79, 81(t,b), 143, 162, 165(b)
Macpherson, Duncan, Artist: 42
Metropolitan Toronto Reference Library: 7, 12, 14, 15, 16, 18, 20, 26, 28, 30, 34(t,b), 36 (il,ir), 39, 43, 44, 50, 66, 71, 77, 85, 87, 88, 89(t,b), 90(t), 92, 94, 95, 101,102, 103, 105, 108, 110, 112, 120, 121, 122, 123, 124, 126, 127, 128, 129, 130, 132, 131, 133, 137, 139, 140, 141, 142, 144, 147, 158, 159, 165(t)
Michigan Historical Collection: 100, 145(b)
Michigan Technology University: 145(t)
Minnesota Historical Society: 104
Missouri Historical Society, St. Louis: 10
Mole, Clarence: 27
National Archives (Washington): 125
National Archives of Canada: 4, 37, 78, 96(b), 106
Parry Sound Public Library: 152, 156
Rindlisbacher, Peter, Marine Artist: 40
Smithsonian Institute: 145(b),
Thunder Bay Historical Society: 163(t,b)
University of Detroit Mercy ( Fr. Edward J. Dowling, S. J. Marine Historical Coll.): 136
Welland Historical Museum: 48
BOOKS
Snider, C.H.J., "Schooner Days," *Toronto Telegram*, Jan 10, 1953: 80
Cook, Samuel F., *Drummond Island, the Story of the British Occupation 1815–1828*(Lansing: R. smith Printing Co.), 1896: 90(b), 91,
Osborne, A.C. "The Migration of Voyageurs from Drummond Island to Penetanguishene in 1828" *Ontario Historical Society Papers and Records, Vol III.* (Toronto: Ontario Historical Society), 1901: 96(t), 97
*Frank Leslie's Illustrated Newspaper*, April 2, 1887: 21

## Acknowledgements

I am deeply grateful to the partners of Lynx Images Inc. for entrusting me with this and previous projects. Special thanks to Barbara Chisholm for exceptional editing and encouragement, to Russell Floren for project producing and picture research, and to Andrea Gutsche for her wonderful design and picture research. Additional thanks to Amy Harkness for her skill in copy editing and Marie Fernandes for proofreading.

# Award-Winning Great Lakes Books and Films From Lynx Images

## MYSTERIOUS ISLANDS
### Forgotten Tales of the Great Lakes

*Mysterious Islands* is an adventurous historical journey to islands found within the vast basin of the five Great Lakes. Standing removed and alone, islands have been central to some of the most important, outrageous, and tragic events in Great Lakes history, from a decisive and bloody naval battle in the War of 1812, to Prohibition rumrunning, to harrowing tales of shipwreck and rescue. The waves of time have left many islands behind, but remnants of the past still mark their shores—burial grounds, grand hotels, abandoned quarries, lighthouses, strategic forts, and even a castle.

THE BOOK includes over 100 stories and over 500 rare photographs and helpful maps. THE VIDEO takes viewers to beautiful and intriguing places through remarkable cinematography and compelling archival footage and images.

*Film Number 2 on the PBS Home Video Bestseller List*

### MORE GREAT LAKES HISTORY WITH LYNX IMAGES...

Since 1988, Lynx Images has been exploring and documenting vanishing pieces of Great Lakes history. Our filmmakers and writers search out fascinating stories, characters and photographs—clues to the Great Lakes' rich and dramatic past.

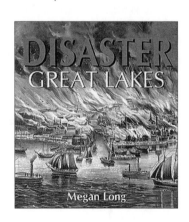

DISASTER GREAT LAKES
(book)
SUPERIOR: Under the Shadow of the Gods
(book and film)
ALONE IN THE NIGHT:
Lighthouses of Georgian Bay & North Channel
(book and film)
THE NORTH CHANNEL AND
ST. MARY'S RIVER
(book)
GHOSTS OF THE BAY:
The Forgotten History of Georgian Bay
(book and film)

For a full catalogue, log on to our web site: www.lynximages.com

# LYNX ⟳ TIME...
## LYNX ⟳ PLACE...
### LYNX ⟳ IMAGES...

Lynx Images is a unique Canadian company that creates books and films filled with engaging stories and dramatic images from Canada's history.

Lynx projects are journeys of discovery, expeditions to sites where the past still resonates.

The company is comprised of a small, dedicated group of writers and film-makers who believe that history is something for all of us to explore.

---

## CANADIAN AUTHORS                    CANADIAN STORIES

### MEGAN LONG

Lynx Images seeks out authors who tell Canadian stories in an engaging way. Our talented researchers and writers have created several best-selling books and award-winning films.

*Ghosts of the Great Lakes* is author Megan Long's second collaboration with Lynx Images. Released in 2002, her previous title, *Disaster Great Lakes*, has received wide interest throughout the region. Long recently moved from Toronto to Vancouver, B.C., where she is enjoying sailing, rock climbing and exploring the history of the West Coast.

---

### JOIN THE ADVENTURE!

We are searching out powerful archival photographs, film footage, knowledgeable contacts, and stories from Canada's past for our future projects, *Childhood Canada* and *bootlegging on the Great Lakes*. We welcome your input and comments. Please mail, fax, or e-mail us at input@lynximages.com

---

## COMMITTED TO A FUTURE OF BRINGING YOU
## MORE OF THE PAST

*Thank you for your support*
—Russell Floren, Barbara Chisholm, Andrea Gutsche
**WWW.LYNXIMAGES.COM**